Engaging the Word

Engaging the Word

The New Testament and the Christian Believer

Jaime Clark-Soles

WESTMINSTER
JOHN KNOX PRESS
LOUISVILLE · KENTUCKY

© 2010 Jaime Clark-Soles

First edition
Published by Westminster John Knox Press
Louisville, Kentucky

10 11 12 13 14 15 16 17 18 19—10 9 8 7 6 5 4 3 2 1

Scripture quotations are from the New Revised Standard Version of the Bible, copyright © 1989 by the Division of Christian Education of the National Council of the Churches of Christ in the U.S.A., and used by permission.

Book design by Sharon Adams
Cover design by Eric Walljasper

Library of Congress Cataloging-in-Publication Data

Clark-Soles, Jaime, 1967–
    Engaging the Word : the New Testament and the Christian believer / Jaime Clark-Soles.
        p. cm.
    Includes indexes.
    ISBN 978-0-664-23114-9 (alk. paper)
    1. Bible. N.T.—Hermeneutics.   I. Title.
    BS2331.C53 2010
    225.6'01—dc22

                                                                    2010017883

PRINTED IN THE UNITED STATES OF AMERICA

⊗ The paper used in this publication meets the minimum requirements
of the American National Standard for Information Sciences—Permanence
of Paper for Printed Library Materials, ANSI Z39.48-1992.

Westminster John Knox Press advocates the responsible use of our natural resources.
The text paper of this book is made from 30% postconsumer waste.

For Chloe and Caleb

Contents

Acknowledgments

This book has been some years in the making and has left me indebted to a number of people. A wise mentor once informed me: "No institution is the kingdom of God." True. But Perkins School of Theology at Southern Methodist University has been a wonderfully supportive place for me to teach, write, and learn for the past decade. Deans William B. Lawrence and Richard Nelson have been supportive of my work. I was fortunate to receive a Perkins Scholarly Outreach Award to write this book. Of course, it's the students of Perkins to whom I am most grateful as they and I continue to study and learn all we can about the New Testament together.

I was privileged to participate in a group devoted to Teaching Biblical Exegesis in Theological Schools (TBETS), led by Matthew Skinner and Christine Yoder and funded by the Wabash Center for Teaching and Learning in Theology and Religion. We met for two weeks in 2006–2007, and I continue to depend heavily upon the wisdom of this group as I ponder pedagogical issues. In addition to Matt and Christine, the group includes Margaret Aymer, Greg Carey, Clayton Croy, Jae Won Lee, Esther Menn, Anathea Portier-Young, Andreas Schuele, Brent Strawn, and Carolyn J. Sharp.

What to say about my dear friend and colleague Carolyn J. Sharp without becoming maudlin? We went to seminary together at Yale Divinity School and earned our PhDs together at Yale University. If it were okay to have idols, she'd be mine. She is exceedingly brilliant, deeply faithful, honest, creative, courageous, and generous. She cares immensely about teaching anyone who wants to learn about the Bible. If it weren't for her, you wouldn't be holding this book. She dreamed up her volume *Wrestling the Word: The Hebrew Scriptures and the Christian Believer* with Jon Berquist. It was decided that a New

Testament companion volume would be in order, and I was invited to write it. I am profoundly grateful to call her friend and colleague.

Jon Berquist is a fine editor, but more important, a wonderful human being. I have likened him to a personal trainer of the best sort: one who pulls out of you the potential within in ways you might not achieve on your own. Thanks, Jon, for your hard work on my behalf. And thanks to the whole team at WJK who invested their valuable time in my book.

My research assistants Jarrod Neal and Michelle Morris deserve mention. Michelle devoted serious time and attention to this volume and saved me from some pitfalls. I am grateful to Rev. Michael Redmond for reading and responding to some of the chapters. Dr. Mark Chancey was especially helpful to me on the historical Jesus chapter. Dr. Paul Anderson provided useful comments on the Synoptic Problem and historical Jesus chapters. Dr. Matthew Skinner shared his wonderful PowerPoint lecture on the Synoptic Problem with me.

A word of thanks is due to the Amarillo Lay School folk who allowed me to engage them in conversation about this book over a two-day period.

My church, Church in the Cliff, continually nourishes and challenges me. It's the closest thing to the kingdom of heaven, the reign of God, I've experienced thus far.

My gym community, led by our trainer Kurtis Register, keeps me grounded year after year and enlarges my vision of my readership. They remind me that working hard and playing hard both matter; when all goes well, work and play become indistinguishable. Better than most, they understand and honor the fact that we do indeed "have this treasure in clay jars" (2 Corinthians 4:7). Thanks, then, to Ron Washington, Mary Ann Harris, Julie England, Richard Schulze, Keith Liljestrand, and Christina Melendez.

Two friends deserve special mention for patiently accompanying me through the writing process and letting me think out loud about the various subjects in this book for which I am so passionate. They are Teri Walker and Keith Liljestrand.

Finally, my wonderful, understanding, supportive, loving family—Thad, Chloe, and Caleb—I love and appreciate you beyond all telling of it.

1

Packaging the Word of God in America Today

Do you ever feel that the Bible is "too big and freaky looking"? Are you ever too intimidated to read it? *Revolve* is for you. It's a **Bible** that looks like a fashion magazine! With this **relevant** format and over 500 further-study notes, you'll feel **comfortable** exploring the Scriptures. Features Include: Blabs (Q & A) . . . , Love Notes from God, Issue articles, Basics of Christianity Articles, Quizzes, Beauty Secrets, Relationship articles, Devotional Reading Plans, and more![1]

So reads the product description of the 2009 *Revolve Bible*, a product created just for girls aged eight to twelve. That's quite a specific market. And the *Revolve Bible* does not fail to deliver on its promise of beauty secrets. Take page 4, for example. Right next to the story of Herod's Slaughter of the Innocents, the murdering of all male children aged two and under, with Rachel's lamentation from the Old Testament, you will find "emergency pimple repair." Apparently, if you rub deodorant on your zits before bed, they will be gone by the morning of Prom. What does this have to do with Matthew 2? Well, as the text says, "Blemishes come and go, but God's Word remains forever."[2]

As a representative example of the trend in Bible products, the *Revolve Bible* provokes a number of observations and questions. First, it claims to be a Bible, when it actually contains only the New Testament. For Christians, the New Testament does not constitute a Bible; this fact appears to be lost

---

1. *Revolve: The Complete New Testament*, New Century Version (Nashville: Thomas Nelson, 2007), from the product description, http://www.christianbook.com/Christian/Books/product_slideshow?sku=016483&actual_sku=016483&slide=2&action=Next.
2. *Revolve* 2007, 4.

on publishers and purchasers alike in the current market. One readily finds plenty of freestanding New Testaments or New Testaments plus Psalms and Proverbs, but not freestanding Old Testaments. What does this imply about contemporary notions of canon and the nature of scriptural authority?

Second, incomparable energy is invested in making the Bible "relevant" and "comfortable"? What makes a Bible or a particular passage of the Bible "relevant"? What has the Slaughter of the Innocents to do with zits? Is making the Bible "comfortable" a worthy goal?

Third, what about the *format* of contemporary Bibles? On page 4 of *Revolve 2007* the zit advice grabs the eye more readily than the biblical text, as does the bit about parental favoritism. The most visually boring portion of the page is the biblical text, which enjoys no color or captivating photos.

Fourth, since it takes the form of a fashion magazine, and fashions change, one must buy a new *Revolve Bible* every single year. Cha-ching! The page mentioned above comes from the *Revolve* 2007 edition, but the publisher hopes you'll buy the newest version: "*Revolve* comes of age! The familiar format and look is **refreshed** and **revved up** in this 2008 edition. Girls will be **thrilled** to hear that the **fourth edition** of this best-selling Bible is available with new sidebars, features, and images **but the same Bible text**!"

What is happening to the Bible? In this chapter, I will assess trends in current Bible products, indicating potential promises and pitfalls and raising questions for further thought. I will emphasize three points about current Bible products: (1) They tend toward the hyperspecific; (2) they operate within the strictures of modernist interpretive strategies; and (3) they raise questions about current notions of canon and scriptural authority.

HYPERSPECIFIC FEATURES

The hyperspecific or hyperindividualistic features are first seen at the level of available translations. At the next level, they appear in terms of specific demographics. Finally, they are evident at the level of individual "experts" attached to the products.

Translations

Those who led the Protestant Reformation longed to place Bibles in the hands of the masses; no longer was the Bible to remain the sole property of the elite magisterium who interpreted the text and handed down the definitive conclusions about the texts to the hoi polloi. Luther himself translated the Bible into the German vernacular to make it accessible to ordinary Christians.

Luther might be satisfied to know that a contemporary English-speaking Christian has access to a dizzying number of different English translations and paraphrases. While 2,000 English translations exist if one includes the commentaries over the past 150 years, there are roughly 10 translations that are what publishers call "economically viable." The King James Version still exerts a strong pull. The New Revised Standard Version, used in most main-line seminaries and among moderate to liberal Christians and heavily touted by biblical scholars, constitutes only 1 percent of the market; that is, it has virtually no influence at all upon the current sales market. I recently visited a large Christian bookstore in the Dallas area, and it did not have a single copy of an NRSV translation; the staff had never even heard of it.

The most popular translations include the King James Version, the New King James Version, the New Living Translation, the New International Version (and the TNIV: Today's NIV), the English Standard Version, the Holman Christian Standard Bible (Southern Baptist), the New Century Version, the New American Standard Bible, the Contemporary English Version ("a simplified version of the Bible designed for children and uneducated adults, those defined as at a fourth-grade reading level"), and Peterson's *The Message*.

In advertising, the claim that a particular translation is "literal" appears to increase respect and sales for it. But, of course, there is no such thing as a "literal" translation. All translation is interpretation. Stop, reader, and say this aloud: "All translation is interpretation." Were it not so, we could have one English translation and be done with it. We have so many translations because there are different theological agendas driving each.

The Bible Plus: Study Notes, Life Application, and Other Supplementary Materials

If the meaning of the biblical texts is already narrowed down through a particular translation process, how much more so by the "study notes," commentary, and numerous other extra features provided in current Bible products that are aimed at extremely specific populations? Luther might approve of the publishers who produce inexpensive mass-market Bibles so that every individual *can* own a Bible; but what if every individual doesn't appear to *want* a Bible? Publishers have clearly studied the market and found that hyperindividualizing the Bible may inspire more people to want to purchase a Bible for themselves or as a gift for someone else. There are Bibles based on gender, but only gender as very narrowly (and perhaps problematically) defined. The insights concerning the social construction and deconstruction of gender that are routine in both the academy and popular culture are not even hinted at in the Bible market. There are Bibles for men and Bibles for women; Bibles for girls and Bibles for boys. Within the gender category, there are Bibles by age. So the *Revolve Bible* mentioned above is only for girls aged eight to twelve. There is no feminist Bible (there are a lot of Bibles aimed at women and have "women" in the title, but they are not feminist; usually quite the contrary).

In addition to gender and age, Bibles are sold according to our hobbies, careers, causes, race, ethnicity, and favorite doctrines (*The Apologetics Study Bible*). There's the *Green Bible* for those with ecological concerns and there's the *African American Bible*.

Then there's the sneaky Bible: the *Metal Bible*, whose product description reads: "It's back—now in green and orange metal. Plain, simple—and totally unexpected—this small, plain text NLT Bible *is about giving young adults something unique without directly saying it's for them.* . . . Style-conscious teens will find this **lightweight** compact edition of the Scriptures irresistible" (emphasis added). A lightweight Bible? Hmmmm . . .

There's *The Duct Tape Bible* and *Immerse: the Water-Resistant Bible*. But why own a water-resistant Bible when you can have a fully waterproof Bible in the form of *The Outdoor Bible*? There's even a Bible for ministers, called (drumroll, please) *The Minister's Bible*; among the features it sports "a practical guide to visitation, sample services for weddings, funerals, and baptisms, a step-by-step plan of salvation, [and] quick-find Scripture references to answer tough questions."[3]

And consider *The Soldier's Bible*; if you want to be more specific, you can purchase *The Marine's Bible*; neither *The Soldier's Bible* nor *The Marine's Bible* should be confused with *The American Patriot's Bible*. The former is strictly for those serving in the armed forces while the latter is

> THE ONE BIBLE THAT SHOWS HOW "A LIGHT FROM ABOVE" SHAPED OUR NATION. Never has a version of the Bible targeted the spiritual needs of those who love our country more than The American Patriot's Bible. This extremely unique Bible shows how the history of the United States *connects the people and events of the Bible to our lives in a modern world*. The story of the United States is *wonderfully woven into* the teachings of the Bible and includes a beautiful full-color family record section, memorable images from our nation's history and hundreds of enlightening articles which *complement* the New King James Version Bible text. (emphasis added)[4]

Do the soldier, minister, and teenage girl really need different Bibles?

3. *The KJV Minister's Bible* (Peabody, MA: Hendrickson Publishers [distributor], 2005), from the product description, http://www.christianbook.com/Christian/Books/product?item_no=636481&netp_id=322866&event=EBRN&item_code=WW&view=covers.
4. *The NKJV American Patriot's Bible* (Nashville: Thomas Nelson, 2009), from the product description, http://www.christianbook.com/the-nkjv-american-patriots-bible-hardcover/9781418541538/pd/541538?item_code=WW&netp_id=586083&event=ESRCN&view=details.

Customer review comments of the *Duct-Tape Bible* on Amazon.com include the following:

"With the hundreds of Bible choices available, what makes *The Duct Tape Bible* stand out is its appearance. Some might think having a paperback Bible wrapped in Duct Tape is nothing more than a money-making gimmick, but others might appreciate the visual metaphor that can be both a conversation starter and also a personal reminder that God's Word, even more than the ever-durable duct tape, never fails, is totally reliable, accomplishes its job, and lasts forever."

"Combining this visual object lesson with the readability of the thought-for-thought New Century Version (NCV) makes this a Bible especially suited for teenage boys or others who are not content to remain inside a cushy comfort zone, but are into 'living it' or 'keeping it real,' or rolling up their sleeves and getting busy after leaving the Sunday morning pew."

"Though the Bible doesn't have too many extra features, not even cross-references, it does have a decent overview of the layout of the Bible and how to approach it. It also includes the 'plan of salvation' (how to be right with God) and a 90-Day Overview of the Bible reading plan. Structurally, it flops right open nice and flat, the print's clear, and while it might not have the word-for-word accuracy of translations like the NASB, NKJV, KJV, or ESV, for regular reading rather than intense studying this NCV is a fine choice for a translation. The silver duct tape version speaks to me more than the camouflage version, though I can see how those heavy into spiritual warfare might choose the camouflage version."

Individual Expert Interpreters

So, Bibles are hyperindividualized with respect to the readers; but they are also hyperindividualized with respect to influential individual "expert" interpreters. In *The Maxwell Leadership Bible*, "The Leadership expert, John Maxwell, brings an in-depth look at God's laws for leaders and leadership with this revised and updated edition presenting John's latest refinements of these principles."[5] Reading *The Joyce Meyer's Everyday Bible* is "like having Joyce Meyer sitting next to you, teaching you chapter-by-chapter and

5. *NKJV Maxwell Leadership Bible*, briefcase ed. (Nashville: Thomas Nelson, 2008), from the product description, http://www.christianbook.com/nkjv-maxwell-leadership-bible-briefcase-edition/9780718025274/pd/025274?item_code=WW&netp_id=526608&event=ESRCN&view=details.

precept-by-precept!"[6] You can buy *Charles Stanley's Life Principles Bible* and *John Macarthur's Study Bible* in both the NASB and the NKJV translations. Is this any different from having the magisterium dole out interpretations to you, dear reader? Does such a Bible represent progress or regress in terms of the Reformation's hopes for biblical interpretation?

Groups of "Expert" Interpreters

Some Bibles aim to avoid the problem of a single dominant personality providing definitive interpretations to the reader. Such are the few "scholarly" study Bibles available, such as the *New Interpreter's Bible* or *The Harper Collins Study Bible*. Scholarly Bibles—which include commentary and study notes by those recognized by the professional guild of biblical studies—have virtually no share of the Bible market. To date, the biblical guild appears unable or unwilling to create Bible products that actually appeal to readers. Visually, these Bibles tend to be quite boring; they make little or no attempt at "life application"; they focus almost exclusively upon "what the Bible meant back then" and leave the question of "what the Bible means today" largely to the individual reader.

Two recent projects attempt to overcome the notable failure of scholars to engage a wide audience. The recent publication of *The Voice: New Testament* (there is no published release date for the Old Testament) supposedly represents a collaborative effort "among scholars, pastors, writers, musicians, poets, and other artists. Four key words describe the vision of this project: holistic (considers heart, soul, and mind); beautiful (achieves literary and artistic excellence); sensitive (respects cultural shifts and the need for accuracy); and balanced (includes theologically diverse writers and scholars)."[7] This Bible stems from the Emergent Church, which itself is somewhat postmodern and somewhat postevangelical. *The Voice* claims to involve scholars, typically known as practitioners of biblical criticism, and even lists them first among the collaborators. But note the following dichotomous categories presented in the product description: "Instead of *confining God's Word in the framework of biblical criticism, The Voice*™ highlights the beauty of God's communication

6. Joyce Meyer, *The Joyce Meyer's Everyday Bible* (Nashville: FaithWords, 2006), from the product description, http://www.christianbook.com/meyers-everyday-bible-bonded-leather-burgundy/9780446578257/pd/578258?item_code=WW&netp_id=448857&event=ESRCN&view=details.
7. *The Voice: New Testament* (Nashville: Thomas Nelson, 2008), vii.

Product Description: *"The Voice*™ is the product of the best minds in this emerging generation of Christian leaders. Together they are helping young people fall in love with the Scriptures. **Instead of confining God's Word in the framework of biblical criticism,** *The Voice*™ **highlights the beauty of God's communication to His people.** In *The Voice*™, the voice of God is heard as clearly as when He first revealed His truth. This is the first-ever complete New Testament in *The Voice*™ translation. Writers include Chris Seay, Lauren Winner, Brian McLaren, Greg Garrett, David B. Capes, and others."

to His people."[8] Apparently we biblical critics confine God's Word and fail to highlight its beauty. A strong indictment, indeed.

A new translation is under production by the United Methodist Publishing House, the *Common English Bible*. The New Testament will appear in 2010 and the Old Testament the following year. It involves a team of two hundred translators, readers, and editors; it is ecumenical in scope and the translation team represents that diversity, though no Orthodox scholars appear. Its stated emphasis is "on education and worship in congregations." The team's fourfold promise is as follows: "1. Clarity of language, as in 'plain speaking'; 2. A reliable, genuine, and credible power to transform lives; 3. An emotional expectation to find the love of God; 4. A rational expectation to find the knowledge of God."[9] Will it have wider appeal than previous scholarly editions?

And another question, perhaps for biblical scholars only: Why are we so averse to producing a Bible that actually appeals to people visually and with respect to life application? Consider Eugene Peterson's *The Message*. No one can fault Peterson's erudition, and no one can accuse him of simply wanting to make a fast buck. He actually wants to invite people in—everyone; he doesn't hoard his knowledge and scoff at those who will never read Greek. Do we have to make the Bible so boring, so irrelevant to lived reality? If we do a poor job of marketing to adults, how much more so for children? No one is going to get tenure for providing solid biblical scholarship for children, of course. In fact, generally speaking, the structures of tenure and promotion militate against scholars being useful in the public domain. If we choose to allow these structures to dictate our production, we shouldn't complain that our insights are having no effect on regular churchgoers.

8. From http://www.amazon.com/Voice-Romans-Gospel-According-Paul/dp/0529123614.
9. About the *Common English Bible* (Nashville: United Methodist Publishing House, forthcoming in 2010), http://www.commonenglishbible.com.

MODERNIST INTERPRETIVE STRATEGIES

The history of biblical interpretation can be roughly divided into three categories of interpretive strategies: premodern (500–1500), modern (Enlightenment–20th century), and postmodern.[10] Obviously the periods overlap historically. Postmodern interpretation of the Bible has been conducted for quite some time now, yet modernist reading strategies dominate the American biblical scene. The drive to narrow down the meaning of a text, to reduce the texts to timeless, generic principles; the use of positivistic notions of truth and objectivity; the preoccupation with historical accuracy, scientific validity, archaeological proof—the *facts*, as it were; and the perhaps unjustified optimism in the power of the historical-critical method to bring us to The One Absolute Literal Truth—all of these characterize modernist hermeneutical habits.[11] Two illustrative examples are *The Chronological Bible* and *The Scofield Reference Bible*. The first produces one overarching historical timeline, then chops up the entire Bible passage by passage or even verse by verse, and maps it onto the timeline. So one reads the whole Bible in what these editors consider to be the correct chronological occurrence rather than canonical order. *The Scofield Reference Bible* is also determined by a particular historical timeline rather than canonical categories. While these are extreme cases,[12] they do exemplify the emphasis on historical categories that appears throughout the Bible products.

A concomitant feature of modernist interpretation is the focus on the rational, disembodied brains of individuals rather than readers who are holistic, complex social beings shaped by interpretive communities. From current Bible products, one might imagine that a Christian and her Bible, and maybe Jesus, God, or the Holy Spirit, constitute a full interpretive community. But is it enough to read one's waterproof Bible all alone in one's kayak? And when one is reading alone, does the reader's voice count as much as the commentator's? Why or why not?

What would a postmodern Bible look like? Perhaps it would seek to open up multiple meanings in the text, to provoke questions at every turn and inspire a love for the power, porosity, and polysemy of language. Best-selling Bibles often highlight the fact that they "simplify" the Bible and make it "plain."

10. For a fuller explanation of these categories, see chap. 2.
11. "In broad outline, the critique looks like this: modernism, with its emphasis on reason, insists on resolving and eliminating the differences between people. But this leads, eventually, to coercion, oppression, domination, cruelty, and abuse of one form or another. Anyone who believes in One True Culture—one right way of doing things—is, knowingly or not, a closet tyrant"; Heath White, *Postmodernism 101: A First Course for the Curious Christian* (Grand Rapids: Brazos Press, 2006), 43.
12. Yet they are not strictly modern: they incorporate premodern tendencies as well.

קין משפט
נר מצוה

הא דתניא נסברה לו חבית של תבית בראש גגו
כל פרק ממחמיסין דריס חביסין (לשון קצר)
מטילין ממנו מאן מאן שלש סעודות אומר לאחרים בואו והצילו לכם
ונוטל מלא יסעו נעתין הצילה אימת שהנאכין בכרמלית

מתני׳ שלש מצוות ולד
לח זו מבני המפולש ואפילו לרבי אליעזר
דאמר בעין לדים הני מילי לאוכלין ומשקין
אבל לספר תורה בלד לא
מתני׳ מצילין *מזון ג׳ סעודות הראוי
לאדם לאדם לבהמה לבהמה כיצד
נפלה דליקה בליל שבת מצילין מזון ג׳
סעודות בשחרית מצילין מזון ב׳ סעודות
לעולם מזון סעודות אחת ר׳ יוסי אומר
גמ׳ מכדי בהדדא קמדא נציל טפי אמר
רבא שרינן ליה אתי לכבויי אי אבי אלא הא
דתניא ״נשברה לו חבית בראש גגו מביא
כלי ומניח תחתיה ובלבד שלא יביא
כלי ויקלוט כלי אחר ויצרף התם

כלי אחר ויקלוט כלי אחר ויצרף
לשמור לי׳ דו לו לאן וכי קאתי לא
מבער לקוטו דמינטר שמעיל הבאר
הכא שאול גרף מן מינבר כלי
הא שאול מלא פת הרדאה. **הצול** פת
נקיה כיף ייל פת הרדאה. בא
נקיה נקיה ביי של פת פאמר מעו

ואחרון קן ייסה הנקנה:

אבל לא מציל ליום הכפורים
פירס בתחרותא למעלה
יומם ישן ואלית מסקינן דחטל גמר הא
ומיט תסקינן למעלה דלא יביא כסף

ותתנא דני רבי ישמעאל
עמוד מלאכה כל

רבינו חננאל

אסקנא דהא דכתיב
ושבתה ולתא אל עברה
לשבת נמי מאי
שבות שבו לי
בה אמר אחר
נמו סטה לבה תני

Postmodern interpreters take joy in complexifying the text or noting the regnant complexity already therein. A postmodern Christian Bible might resemble the Jewish Talmud, which in some ways was postmodern before its time.[13]

A page of Talmud has the ancient authoritative text called the Mishnah (2nd century) in the central column along with the earliest commentary, called the Gemara (4th–6th century). This central column is surrounded by the various ideas and interpretations of later commentators across the centuries, no two of whom agree. A Pomo (postmodern) Bible would model different methodological approaches and voices from diverse social locations. Since postmoderns are suspicious of authority, a Pomo Bible would not be dominated by the voice of a single expert or elite group of any kind.

Before the Reformation, interpretation was conducted by trained priestly elites and dispensed to churchgoers. The downside to that, one might argue, is that it did not allow the individual to engage in the interpretive project. On the good side, there was an emphasis on the community. In modern Protestantism, if Bible products and sales are any gauge, we might have Reformation run amok. The Bible is now available to each of us for interpretation, but is there an overemphasis on the individual and the personal customization of the Bible and the faith?

To what degree and in what ways should popular culture be engaged, accommodated, or avoided? This question appears from Genesis to Revelation and applies equally well to the manufacturing and sales of Holy Writ. Do we need to seduce people into reading the Bible? What level of commercialization is appropriate, if any? Is a Bible in the form of a fashion magazine that must be bought anew each year a good idea? What's being sold anyway? Is it harmless, or does it cheapen the Bible to sell it with sets of different covers that you can change to match your purse or shoes?

CANON AND SCRIPTURAL AUTHORITY

A canvassing of current Bible products raises questions about canon and scriptural authority:

1. Why do we buy Bibles and why do we read Bibles?

2. Does the format of our Bibles lead to confusion about what counts as Scripture versus what counts as mere commentary and personal opinion? As noted above, in the Talmud our Jewish brothers and sisters have canonized commentary by printing the ancient Mishnaic text in the center surrounded

13. The previous page from the Talmud is taken from http://commons.wikimedia.org/wiki/File:V12p022a01_Talmud.jpg.

by various, discordant interpretations by authoritative figures over the centuries. To date, Christians have not officially chosen such a strategy. But, de facto, this seems to be happening wherever a Charles Stanley's or a Joyce Meyer's comment on Scripture proves determinative for any Christian reader.

3. How much should we stuff into a Bible itself? How much is too much? Should we have anything in there but the text? Do we *need* zit advice next to the Slaughter of the Innocents? What message does this send about the canonical texts and the nature of their authority? Are the study notes to *complement* the text (as *The American Patriot Bible* claims), to provide *life application*, to *make* the texts relevant, to push toward a particular theology (see *The Scofield Reference Bible*), to propagate the ideas of a particular influential or charismatic contemporary religious figure or a group of such cultural icons, or what?

4. Particularly troubling is the prevalent practice of publishing and circulating freestanding New Testaments or New Testaments plus Psalms and Proverbs. Such a practice implies that the Old Testament is not part of the Christian canon at all or is somehow less canonical and certainly less authoritative than the 27 books of the New Testament. Marcion and company tried this approach in the 2nd century and it was declared heresy; yet publishing houses, even those associated with denominations that emphatically insist that the Bible is infallible and inerrant, regularly follow the Marcionite path. This practice has deep, deleterious, maybe even dangerous theological ramifications.

CONCLUSION

One of the most delightful trends is the production of visual Bibles and audio Bibles. One good audio Bible is *The Bible Experience*, which boasts over 200 African American actors, musicians, and personalities, including Denzel Washington and Cicely Tyson. Every book of the Bible is read dramatically, with different voices for the different characters and no additional commentary.

Let me close by asking: What if we just had Bibles in different translations with no commentary and no study notes whatsoever? What if we congregated around the Bible, read it together in community, and discussed it? We would agree, of course, to read supplemental materials that would aid us in the interpretive process, such as fiction, poetry, movies, history, archaeology, theology, and the daily newspaper, but such material would remain *outside of and separate from the printed Bible* as happens with audio Bible products. Just a Bible and a community and a thirst for knowledge aimed at the love of God.

2

Different Ways of Reading

Promises and Pitfalls

The Word of the Lord: A reading from 1 Corinthians 11:27–32

Whoever, therefore, eats the bread or drinks the cup of the Lord in an unworthy manner will be answerable for the body and blood of the Lord. Examine yourselves, and only then eat of the bread and drink of the cup. For all who eat and drink without discerning the body, eat and drink judgment against themselves. For this reason many of you are weak and ill, and some have died. But if we judged ourselves, we would not be judged. But when we are judged by the Lord, we are disciplined so that we may not be condemned along with the world.

This is the Word of the Lord. Thanks be to God.

What if you went to church next Sunday and the passage above was the text for the day's sermon, with a special focus on verse 30: "For this reason many of you are weak and ill, and some have died." Or what if you were asked to lead a Bible study on it with adults, youth, or children? How would that go for you and your community? Would it strike you as puzzling and requiring some sort of deeper attention? Would people assume that it must be worth studying because it's in Scripture and Scripture is the sacred, authoritative text of the church? Would they feel like it's simply a vestige of ancient Christianity that can be summarily sloughed off by 21st-century Christians?

Or what about Acts 5:1–11, the story of Ananias and Sapphira?

But a man named Ananias, with the consent of his wife Sapphira, sold a piece of property; with his wife's knowledge, he kept back some of

13

the proceeds, and brought only a part and laid it at the apostles' feet. "Ananias," Peter asked, "why has Satan filled your heart to lie to the Holy Spirit and to keep back part of the proceeds of the land? While it remained unsold, did it not remain your own? And after it was sold, were not the proceeds at your disposal? How is it that you have contrived this deed in your heart? You did not lie to us but to God!" Now when Ananias heard these words, he fell down and died. And great fear seized all who heard of it. The young men came and wrapped up his body, then carried him out and buried him.

After an interval of about three hours his wife came in, not knowing what had happened. Peter said to her, "Tell me whether you and your husband sold the land for such and such a price." And she said, "Yes, that was the price." Then Peter said to her, "How is it that you have agreed together to put the Spirit of the Lord to the test? Look, the feet of those who have buried your husband are at the door, and they will carry you out." Immediately she fell down at his feet and died. When the young men came in they found her dead, so they carried her out and buried her beside her husband. And great fear seized the whole church and all who heard of these things.

This is the Word of the Lord. Thanks be to God (?).

Again, what questions would this text raise? How would it be handled?

The Revised Common Lectionary contains neither the Acts nor the 1 Corinthians passages. Do you wonder why? Sure, it contains the "words of institution" from 1 Corinthians 11:23–26:

For I received from the Lord what I also handed on to you, that the Lord Jesus on the night when he was betrayed took a loaf of bread, and when he had given thanks, he broke it and said, "This is my body that is for you. Do this in remembrance of me." In the same way he took the cup also, after supper, saying, "This cup is the new covenant in my blood. Do this, as often as you drink it, in remembrance of me." For as often as you eat this bread and drink the cup, you proclaim the Lord's death until he comes.

The Revised Common Lectionary is a resource for Christian worship published in 1994 that lists for each Sunday four readings: a Psalm, another passage from the Hebrew Bible (or Apocrypha, or Acts), a Gospel lesson, and an Epistle reading (or a reading from Revelation). It is widely used in the United States and Canada, and to some degree in Great Britain. The readings run on a three-year cycle, coded to three of the four Gospels: A–Matthew, B–Mark, and C–Luke. Sadly, no year is devoted to the Gospel of John though some passages appear in various seasons annually.

But there it stops, just before our passage.

So how do we Christians fruitfully engage and interpret such difficult texts? Or any of our sacred texts, for that matter? In this chapter, I will outline premodern, modern, and postmodern biblical approaches. In each case, I will note the potential promises and pitfalls and invite you to do the same.

PREMODERN APPROACHES

Do you remember the song by Supertramp called "The Logical Song"? If not, now would be a good time to download and listen to it. First, it summarizes the premodern, modern, and postmodern epochs in intellectual history in a convenient way. Second, it sketches the spiritual development of a postmodern Christian.

The premodern approach to Scripture generally dates to the period between antiquity and the Enlightenment, so around 500–1500 CE.[1] In shorthand terms, it may be characterized as follows:

- Uncritical
- Unproblematic
- Acceptance of the supernatural realm
- Unquestioned acceptance of the received tradition
- Leaving room for mystery and religious experience

Picture the premodern interpreter singing the first stanza of "The Logical Song": life is "wonderful" and "magical"—it's a "miracle." Let's fill out the picture a bit more. In this era, the government was feudal; power lay in the hands of kings and nobles, and their access to power was set by tradition. Upward social mobility did not exist; one's social position was fixed by birth. Hierarchy in the church structure was no less rigid, and the magisterium dictated the shape and the details of the Christian faith. Literacy rates were quite low as compared to a current rate of 99% in America.[2] Laypeople were not expected to read let alone *interpret* the Bible; that was the job of the church officials. Belief in magic and miracles and what moderns would call "superstition" was assumed. The rituals of church life—baptism, liturgy, Eucharist, and so forth—provided the structure of one's religious life and community.

So when our premodern interpreters heard in 1 Corinthians 11 that some people were getting sick and dying by taking communion in an unworthy

---

1. I am indebted to Heath White's *Postmodernism 101: A First Course for the Curious Christian* (Grand Rapids: Brazos Press, 2006). Note that this presentation tends to refer to activity in Europe.
2. "Field Listing: Literacy," *CIA World Factbook*, https://www.cia.gov/library/publications/the-world-factbook/fields/2103.html.

manner, how would they have heard that? Most probably they would assume that if one takes communion in an unworthy manner, one might get sick and die. God judges. There is a strong separation between "the world," meaning "those people," and the church, meaning "us." But Christians should beware because present membership in the church does not guarantee safety. Excommunication was always an option.

As for Ananias and Sapphira, well, it happened like the Bible says it happened. They shouldn't have lied, and they should have respected the authority of the apostles. But they lied and defied, so they died.

PROMISES AND PITFALLS
OF PREMODERN INTERPRETATION

By modern or postmodern standards, our premodern interpreter might be considered naive with respect to biblical interpretation. He or she interpreted the Bible as the church instructed. There was, however, an immediacy of religious experience, of seeing "signs" of God's action in ordinary life that I'm afraid has been lost or denigrated by the modern mind.

MODERNIST APPROACHES

Modernist approaches date from the Enlightenment to the late 20th century.[3] Using our shorthand, we might note the following:

- Strong confidence in reason and science
- An expectation that education and use of human reason would lead to a harmonious, unified, just, "civilized" world
- Impatient or dismissive of the supernatural realm and, concomitantly, of people or whole cultures who insist on holding on to such "unscientific, irrational superstitions"
- A drive to demythologize the texts and retain only the objective, universal, timeless truths or principles found therein

Filling out the picture, we would need to note some of the key figures and developments that led to the Enlightenment. Famously, in 1517 Martin Luther posted his 95 Theses, which led to the 16th-century Protestant Reformation. With respect to our concern, biblical interpretation, this was a

---

3. Needless to say, historical periods cannot be cleanly dated; we set dates merely for heuristic purposes, realizing that periods overlap and different criteria for dating will produce different results.

watershed moment in history as authority moved from the pope to Scripture. That is to say, Martin Luther declared that the rule of life and faith should be determined *sola scriptura*, by Scripture alone, rather than by the authority of the magisterium. This move was aided by the invention of the printing press by Gutenberg in the 15th century. Luther's commitment to translating the Bible into the vernacular to make it available for individual Christians to read must be noted and perhaps praised.

In terms of scientific developments (which always affect developments in biblical interpretation), recall the work of Copernicus (1543), Galileo (1610), and Newton (1686), which overturned the established Aristotelian worldview and placed Earth at the center of the universe. The realization that Earth and human beings are literally not the center of the universe had far-reaching effects upon every aspect of conceptualizing human life.

In terms of biblical interpretation, the Enlightenment brought the advent of rational biblical criticism, most notably inaugurated by Reimarus and others who produced a genre of literature called "Lives of Jesus" in which they sought to subject the biblical accounts of Jesus to the scrutiny of rational "scientific" critique. Those parts of the tradition that were considered irrational or mythological were questioned. Miracles were dismissed or explained away. In place of Jesus' walking on water, critics reasoned that he actually found a sandbar on which to stand such that he only *appeared* to be walking on water. These initial, entertaining soundings eventually developed into what is known as the historical-critical method, which until recently was the primary method used and taught in mainline seminaries. We'll address that in a moment.

Biblical scholars have come up with a useful threefold schema that envisions the world "behind" the text, the world "within" the text, and the world "in front of" the text. The "world behind the text" refers to the original 1st-century world in which the New Testament texts were produced. To understand that world, we have to ask about the social, economic, and political structures and realities of that time. What was it like to live under the Roman Empire? How did the education system work? How did people travel? How long did people live? Who had status and who didn't? What kind of art was produced? Was there birth control? How did medicine work? What were attitudes about gender, sexuality, philosophy, religion, politics, family, and so on?

The "world within the text" refers to the text itself, from the opening verse to the final verse. If we are studying a Gospel, we ask questions about narrative, questions about plot, setting, character, themes, language, metaphor, imagery, point of view, and conflict. We use methods of narrative and literary criticism. If we are studying an epistle, we use rhetorical criticism and note how the text relies on common rhetorical techniques of the time. For instance, Paul's letters typically open with reference to the sender and the recipient, followed by a thanksgiving section, and the body of the letter in which he employs various speech techniques, depending upon the rhetorical aims of that particular letter.

The "world-in-front-of the text" refers to what we call the "reception-history" (*Rezeptionsgeschichte*)[4] of the text or "the history-of-effects" (*Wirkungs-geschichte*) of the text. How have the texts been received and used over the centuries that follow? How have they influenced art, society, government, economics, science? We know, for instance, that certain texts in the New Testament, such as John 8, have had dire consequences for Jewish-Christian relations over the centuries. We know that texts like Ephesians 5 and 1 Peter 2 were used by pro-slavery advocates to keep slavery legal and "ordained by God." We know that many people base their views concerning issues such as homosexuality or women's leadership in the church upon particular biblical passages. The history of effects that these texts have had globally over the centuries is an important area of study; a number of different methods are employed in studying those effects, from political history, to psychology, art history, cultural studies, anthropology, gender studies, postcolonial studies, and deconstructionism—to name just a few.

The historical-critical method aims to help the interpreter understand the world "behind" the text: the original context in which the scriptural texts were written. It asks, "What did the original author intend to convey through the text to the original audience in the 1st century?" In truth, the method is a conglomeration of methods: textual criticism, form criticism, source criticism, and redaction criticism. Let me say a word about each.

Textual criticism is the branch of study that reviews our some 5,000 ancient New Testament texts and fragments of texts (as well as ancient translations and quotations from the NT) and attempts to provide the most likely original wording of those texts. We have no autographs: that is, we have *no* original New Testament texts. Our earliest fragments of New Testament texts date to the 2nd century. The earliest complete New Testament we have dates from the 4th century, more than 300 years after Jesus' death. The textual critics among us pore over all of these ancient scraps, argue with one another over the most probable original readings, and then produce a Greek New Testament. They also provide a book (see Metzger's *Textual Commentary on the Greek New Testament*) that outlines the main issues and why they chose a particular reading for that edition (we are now using the 27th edition of the Nestle-Aland Greek New Testament, by the way).[5] Text critics operate

4. For a fuller explication of this concept, see "Reception Theory," in Richard N. Soulen and R. Kendall Soulen, *Handbook of Biblical Criticism* (Louisville, KY: Westminster John Knox Press, 2001), 158.

5. Eberhard and Erwin Nestle, Barbara and Kurt Aland, et al., eds., *Novum Testamentum Graece*, 27th ed. (Stuttgart: Deutsche Bibelgesellschaft, 1993, with later, corrected printings).

by a very particular, detailed set of theories and practices that attend to the various dates, geographical factors, and scribal tendencies related to the transmission of these texts. So when your New Testament professor holds up a Greek New Testament, it's not as though we have an actual 1st-century, or even 2nd-, 3rd-, or 4th-century text that it mimics. It is a scholarly construct. From there, English speakers then produce a myriad of English translations guided by particular agendas. I do not use the word "agenda" pejoratively here; I simply want to note that there are many different translation theories at work and many different doctrinal stances, all of which influence the choices that the translators make. The reader of any English translation must remain aware that many choices have already been made for them, many meanings determined, all of which may be open to question and debate.[6]

Form critics study the individual units of New Testament texts that circulated in oral form before the stage of composition, that is in the period between Jesus' death around 30 CE, and the writing of the New Testament around 50–125. They argue that these individual units that circulated orally before the writing of the Gospels reveal the church's activity in its earliest years: evangelizing, preaching, teaching, baptizing, worshiping, serving Eucharist, exhorting, ministering to those in need—much like what the church is still up to today. We see lodged in our current texts older material that circulated earlier, such as hymns (see Phil. 2:6–11; Col. 1:15–20), baptismal formulas (see Gal. 3:27–28), miracle stories, parables, Passion narratives.

Redaction critics realize that at some point certain Christians decided that these traditions should be gathered together into a narrative whole and committed to writing; hence, the birth of a new genre of literature, Gospels. Typically, Gospels narrate the prebirth, birth, life, death, resurrection, postresurrection appearances, and ascension of Jesus, though most do not contain all of those elements. The Gospel writers took it upon themselves to edit their inherited materials and shape them into a unified whole that was useful for their own congregations who were meeting around 70–100, about 40 to 70 years after Jesus' crucifixion, though each of the four differ from one another in certain ways. To study this level of the tradition, historical critics use the method of *redaction criticism* to ferret out the theological intentions of each Gospel author by paying particular attention to the ways they edited the

---

6. For a good read on the various translations both ancient and modern, see Bruce M. Metzger, *The Bible in Translation: Ancient and English Versions* (Grand Rapids: Baker Academic, 2001). I like this because it proceeds chronologically, which helps readers see who was reacting to what when they devised new English translations. For a useful book on the translation process, translation theory, and what is gained or lost by different approaches, see Steven M. Sheeley and Robert N. Nash, *The Bible in English Translation: An Essential Guide* (Nashville: Abingdon Press, 1997). Also see Steven M. Sheeley and Robert N. Nash, *Choosing a Bible: A Guide to Modern English Translations and Editions* (Nashville: Abingdon Press, 1999).

materials each had at hand in composing their Gospels. Redaction critics see the Gospel writers as creative authors who shape the material rather than as mere "stringers of pearls" who clumsily and artlessly paste together various received traditions. They are authors in their own right, and each singularly presents the material.

But where did the Gospel writers, not to mention Paul, who wrote decades earlier (in the 50s), get their material? Those interested in this question engage in *source criticism*. We will have much more to say about this in the chapter on the Synoptic Problem.

The *historical-critical method* emphasizes authorial intention; it assumes that the author had a clear intention and that it is recoverable to a certain degree by using the tools of the historian. Not surprising for a method that grew out of the Enlightenment, with its focus upon the genius of the individual, this method tends to imagine an individual (usually male) author composing largely alone (much as a scholar does when writing a book like this), with a particular audience in mind as the recipient. The historical critic understands the primary task to be recovering and reconstructing that process in an effort to understand its meaning in the past. The focus is on what the text *meant* then, not what the text *means* now.

Historical critics will first want to learn the languages in which the original texts were written: Hebrew for the Old Testament and Greek for the New Testament. This is known as *philological study*. They will want to understand and privilege what Paul, the Pharisaic Jew, meant when he used the term "faith" or "righteousness" or "salvation" instead of what the word might mean to a modern Lutheran or Catholic or Baptist. In other words, ideally interpreters will lay aside their own theological convictions and "simply let the text speak." They will do this by learning about ancient forms of Judaism and using a concordance to locate each place such a term appears in the Old Testament (Paul's and Jesus' scriptural texts) and in Paul's letters, in order to construct a sense of his meaning for each concept.

Modernist historians aim to objectively analyze the historical data, to reconstruct the past "as it actually happened." Personal biases should not cloud the issues or predetermine the outcome. If apparent contradictions arise in the historical record, they should be analyzed and adjudicated if possible; certainly they should not be swept under the rug in an effort to provide a seamless picture of the evidence. For example, if Matthew indicates that Jesus was born in the time of Herod the Great, and we know that Herod the Great died in 4 BCE, then the historian will be puzzled by Luke's indication that Jesus was born when Quirinius was governor of Syria in 6 CE. What are we to do about the 10-year discrepancy? Historically speaking, both cannot be "true." Likewise, Jesus dies on a different day in the Gospel of John than he does in the Synoptic Gospels (Matthew, Mark, and Luke). By the time he's conducting the Last Supper in the Synoptics, he's already dead in John.[7] And there are countless other examples of historical contradictions or puzzles that we could adduce. Historical critics boldly raise these issues and force us to consider the data and attempt to explain all of it using the tools of rational inquiry.

Thanks to the scholars of Greek and Roman history (classicists), we know much about the social history of the New Testament era. We have a sense of the political, social, economic, and religious structures of the time. We can imagine, as one famous New Testament scholar puts it, what is was like "to be an ordinary Christian in the time of Paul."[8] We do this by reading all of the available material from antiquity: Jewish, Christian, pagan, medical texts, blessing and curse tablets, philosophical treatises, legal documents, political speeches, graffiti, high literature, folk literature, ancient novels, dream interpretations, biographies of famous people—every piece of writing on paper (well, technically, papyrus and parchment), stone, or pottery that has been found. In addition to writings, we analyze every piece of material culture discovered and processed by archaeologists in order to reconstruct the life of ancient citizens.

New Testament scholars also routinely draw upon the work of both sociologists and anthropologists under the assumption that what we learn about modern groups and cultures might apply more or less to our ancient brothers and sisters as well. For example, in modern America one gains status through material wealth and conspicuous consumption. In contrast, the ancient Mediterranean world, the setting for the New Testament, maintained an honor/shame culture that operated according to principles quite foreign to the modern American eye. Many cultures today also operate on an honor/shame basis, so New Testament scholars are keen to read studies by sociologists and anthropologists that explain and delineate the shape of such societies in ways that seem applicable to ancient societies as well. In such a society, social relations operate by strict codes concerning how honor and shame are attained; this is especially true with respect to class and gender.

The modernist approach to the Bible, then, insists that the text be subjected to historical, scientific, rational analysis so that we can lay bare what the original author intended to convey to the original audience by means of the text. Only interpretations that remain within the bounds of historical plausibility and authorial intent gain a hearing. Our modernist interpreter is represented well by the next part of "The Logical Song": "logical," "practical," "clinical." The modern period (18th–late 20th century) placed its eggs in the basket of reason that marks the philosophical, political, and scientific

7. Felix Just has composed a useful chart that lays this out for you beautifully at http://catholic-resources.org/Bible/Jesus-Death.htm.

8. Wayne A. Meeks, *First Urban Christians* (New Haven, CT: Yale University Press, 1983).

activity of the time. Politically, there was a turn to the rights of the individual and democracy. Unbridled optimism abounded. Since human beings are rational animals, we would simply educate everyone; then we would apply rational, scientific principles to all areas of life and we would, as reasonable people using these objective methods of inquiry, all agree. We would create peaceful, just societies where all sing in perfect harmony—or at least refrain from routinely slaughtering one another.

The modernist confidence in the power of science and reason to save us from our sins has been severely chastened. On a small scale, take the historical-critical method, a scientific, unbiased method of exegeting Scripture that supposedly moves our own biases out of the way and "lets the text speak for itself." Why, then, do scholars who use the same so-called scientific method routinely arrive at diametrically opposed conclusions?

On a large scale, there's the ongoing slaughter. We slaughtered each other more in the 20th century than ever before, though science and reason taught us how to do it much more efficiently. "In broad outline, the critique looks like this: modernism, with its emphasis on reason, insists on resolving and eliminating the differences between people. But this leads, eventually, to coercion, oppression, domination, cruelty, and abuse of one form or another. Anyone who believes in One True Culture—one right way of doing things—is, knowingly or not, a closet tyrant."[9]

Enter postmodernism. But before turning to that, let's ask how our modernist interpreter would handle the 1 Corinthians and Acts passages. The modernist interpreter of 1 Corinthians 11 would read the text in Greek and ask about the sociohistorical context of the passage. He (rarely she) would ask about Jewish and Hellenistic beliefs regarding ritual eating and magical notions. He would demythologize the text by noting that we post-Enlightenment moderns do not believe that people die from taking communion incorrectly. He would say something like this: "Some people were sick and dying so Paul used that fact to argue backward from that to locate the cause in communion practices." At any rate, modernist interpretation would peel away the ancient, superstitious, prescientific medical, magical notions and turn attention to other parts of the Communion supper, such as how the rich were mistreating the poor. This is the move the lectionary makes. I find the lectionary to be a great example of modernist biblical assumptions; note its penchant for excising elements that appear parochial, uncivilized, untoward, and offensive to modern, rational, educated sensibilities.

The modernist interpreter would also dispense with the magical notions in Acts 5 and instead look for what it tells us about how the ancient community

9. White, *Postmodernism 101*, 43.

was structured and so on. More likely, the modernist would move on to a more rational text that could speak to a reasonable person. Modernist approaches generally "explain away" the miraculous and force the texts to conform to a scientific, materialist worldview. By "materialist," I mean a view that accepts as fact only what is available to the five senses.

PROMISES AND PITFALLS
OF MODERNIST APPROACHES

Modernist approaches are beneficial in that they force us to draw out and honor the original meaning of the text in its original context so that we don't simply make the texts mean whatever we want them to mean. Drawing the original meaning out is known as *exegesis*, from the Greek *ek* (out) plus *hēgeomai* (lead)," which in this context adds up to "explain." Reading whatever meaning one likes into the text without attention to or regard for its original historical context is known as *eisegesis*, from Greek *eis* (into) plus *hēgeomai* (lead). While there may be no single correct interpretation, historical criticism provides a spectrum of more and less reasonable interpretations, better and worse. Furthermore, certain aspects of human existence seem to be timeless and universal; historical analysis can show connections between present and past.

My first-semester seminary students often find the fruits of historical-critical inquiry both disturbing and liberating simultaneously. Ironically, modernist criticism of the Bible can be disturbing patently because the students have been taught to think in modernist categories: that is, for something to be "true," it must be linear, rational, noncontradictory, and historically, scientifically accurate. So if the Synoptics say that Jesus cleansed the temple at the end of his ministry but John says it happened at the start of his ministry, both cannot be "true." And if one thing in the Bible is proved to be "untrue," then how do we know that anything in it is true? And if we don't know which parts are true, then how can we "trust" the Bible? And if we can't "trust" the Bible, then what is our knowledge and faith based upon? Is it all just sinking sand?

On the other hand, most of my seminary students are thinking Christians, and they noticed some of these issues before they ever came to seminary. But they found that when they raised them in their church, they were seen as complicated people who "overanalyze," "just don't have enough faith," or at worst are insubordinate heretics. For them, coming together with others to dig deeply into the critical issues surrounding biblical interpretation is challenging, but life giving. It helps them to make much more sense of the Bible and its contents, and they discover that they may have been sold a bill of goods or at least just settled for much less than they should have with respect to the wonderful, transformative potential that exists for thoughtful Christians who apply themselves to the serious but delightful task of critical biblical interpretation. Sure, it may be that for a while the Bible that once seemed as familiar as the back of their hand now becomes somewhat foreign as it is placed back in its original 1st-century context, where people thought quite differently from us in a number of ways. But that same phenomenon allows them to read the Bible with fresh eyes and so to be addressed by it in new ways. They are delighted to discover that their mind is a tool of faith rather than its enemy, that Christianity is more than just a nice, warm feeling or matter of the heart. As the blessed apostle Paul commands: "Do not be conformed to this world, but be transformed by the renewing of your *minds*, so that you may discern what is the will of God—what is good and acceptable and perfect" (Romans 12:2).

We should be aware, though, that even the historian will not escape his or her cultural categories and will, therefore, overlay them onto the investigation. The notion that one's interpretation is "objective" or "scientific" may turn out to be unaware at best, disingenuous at worst. In addition, historians may tend to overidentify modernity with antiquity and wrongly assume that categories we use also apply to antiquity.

As some Bible professors like to say, their job involves making the Bible seem both familiar *and* strange. That is, for those who have loved and relied upon the Bible their whole lives, it can be hard to hear a fresh, scandalous, or convicting word from it because the reader assumes she already knows what it all means: whatever she has learned in her church Bible study over the years. These students are often helped by learning that the Bible really was produced in a culture different from our own and that fact should not be overlooked.

On the other hand, some students show up to class with little or no prior experience with the Bible, so that the Bible seems so foreign and strange and distant that it's hard for them to imagine (a) confidently interpreting it with respect to its original context and (b) confidently interpreting it in a meaningful way for the church today. They may wonder how something written "way back then" in a faraway place and time could have any real authority for the lives of modern Christians. Historical-critical methodology, though, shows that the tools with which students are already familiar from studying other literature can be fruitfully and faithfully applied to Scripture. Scripture did not fall out of the sky of a piece. It was written by real Christians living in actual historical places. Such students often discover that our ancient brothers and sisters struggled with many of the same issues we do today, to the degree that their experience illumines our own. After all, Christians believe in a God who has always acted in history in very particular ways and will continue to do so. The Christian God is not aloof and distant, but involved in the messiest details of human history as a whole and the lives of each individual within it.

POSTMODERN APPROACHES

Postmodern approaches developed as a reaction to the premises, and what some considered the excesses, of modernism. Postmodernism dates from the 1960s to the present and can be characterized as follows:

- always questioning
- suspicious of authority
- highly attuned to power dynamics among individuals, societies, and cultures
- wary of any project that seeks to eliminate differences
- extremely attentive to the ways language is used, since language creates realities
- marked by epistemological humility: we don't know as much as we pretend to know
- views the world through an ironic lens: things are not as they appear
- eschews notions of ABSOLUTE TRUTH in order to defend truth
- notions of truth are less like Stonehenge (solid, monolithic, unchanging, hard) and more like Etch-a-Sketch (fluid, sketchy, diverse, subject to revision as more information or news is revealed)

The postmodern interpreter would identify strongly with this part of "The Logical Song": "Won't you please, please tell me what we've learned; I know it sounds absurd, but please tell me who I am."[10] Postmoderns do not find differences among human beings and cultures a "problem" to be resolved. They delight in difference and, at their best, extend hospitality and respect to the Other, treating them as one's equal rather than a mind to be colonized by one's own convictions. They know that they can best come to understand themselves by dialoguing with the Other. This often makes them brave in engaging Bible passages that are "out there" from a modernist perspective. To my mind, they are like the X-gamers of biblical interpretation; they seek out the extremes in order to max out their potential development.

Anyone who refuses to assimilate or blindly to participate in groupthink or be a "model citizen" is threatening and should expect criticism. Jesus had this problem, as did the apostles after him. They would understand these lyrics:

---

10. Supertramp, "The Logical Song," *Breakfast in America* (A & M Records, 1979), available several places online (you can Google it).

"Now watch what you say or they'll be calling you a radical, liberal, fanatical, criminal. Won't you sign up your name? We'd like to feel you're acceptable, respectable, presentable, a vegetable!" We see what choice they made.

When our postmodern interpreter reads 1 Corinthians 11, she will wonder what kinds of questions it raises for the interpretive community. She will want to know where God is in the passage and what it means for the way we do life and community. Do we really think that we'll die if we take communion in an unworthy manner? What does this text say about God's nature? I was always taught that God was hiding in the bushes, waiting to zap me for any mistake. Is this true? And what does it say about the community? How does one discern the body? What *is* the body? Do we really see ourselves as separate from the world? Aren't we part of it? What is it that God condemns, and why is the world condemned if God created it? A conversation would ensue, and each contribution would be considered and would push to further questions and points of agreement and disagreement, with no actual punch line declared by the pastor or teacher two minutes before it's time to go. The same would happen with the Ananias and Sapphira passage.

Because I have chosen two particularly difficult biblical texts for this chapter, the reader may get the impression that all of this interpretive work is needed only for the hard stuff we encounter in our texts. Such is not the case—it applies to each and every passage.

Emergent Churches as a Postmodern Case Study

You may have heard of a recent trend in Christianity referred to as "the emergent movement." It consists largely of postmodern postevangelicals who are rediscovering the value of ancient practices while creatively contributing new ones, especially in embodied ways that engage all the senses and with an emphasis on art. Indeed, many denominations now have an emergent arm (Luthermergent, Presbymergent, Anglimergent, etc.) and the movement is thriving internationally (see http://www.emergentvillage.com). Participants tend to be people conversant with and heavily influenced by a postmodern worldview, though they differ from their secular counterparts in a number of ways. In what follows I want to sketch some characteristic features of these emerging approaches to Scripture in order to flesh out my description of postmodern interpretation and to familiarize readers with this current trend. I will present emergents at their best and, of course, in oversimplified terms given the brevity of my presentation.

Emerging churches are not seeker churches; emergents tend to have been formed in churches where the Bible is front and center, so they are familiar with the stories. When you delve into the meaning of a passage with them, they are likely to say, "Well, I was always taught that the moral of that story was such-and-such." That is, they tend to be formed in communities where the goal of biblical interpretation is to *narrow* the meaning ideally to one point rather than to open it up and glory in the many possible layers and angles. Where so-called Bible-believing churches (BBCs) strive for univocality, emergents are drawn to polyvalence; where the BBCs try to simplify the text, emergents complexify. Both will tell you they aren't *making* the text simple (for the BBCs) or complex (for the emergents); the text itself *is* simple, or complex.

Emergents tend toward *hopeful irony* and *serious play*. They relish paradox, and this often gives them eyes to see and ears to hear because irony is a key feature of the Bible, the gospel, and the life of faith. God's power is made perfect in weakness? Losing your life to find it? Dying to live? A crucified messiah? The likes of you and me as God's hands and feet? Ironic.

Their sense of irony breeds hope and joy, not despair and cynicism. I think it's because they take God very seriously and themselves less seriously. That seems like the right proportion to me. They readily understand that we have this treasure in clay jars and they aren't wracked with guilt over it. God appears actually to enjoy human beings, so why hate our weaknesses and why pretend? Prima donnas and sanctimonious types do not fare well among emergents. Remember the *pneumatikoi* in the Corinthian church? The spiritual know-it-alls? Emergents have as much patience with them as Paul did.

Emergents note that Jesus took special interest in those whose lives were an obvious mess. So when they approach the text, they don't fear the ugly parts—they shine a spotlight on them and ask what they can tell us about God's work in the world and our lives. How do those texts move us toward hope, and in what ways do they implicate us as a community and as individuals?

The Bible is *iconic* for emergents; that is, it makes God visible, but it is not God. It makes Christ visible, but it is not Christ; it makes the work of the Spirit visible, but it is not the Spirit. It is a sign, and signs point to things; they are not the thing itself. When the icon is taken for the thing it's signifying, it becomes an idol. Thus, emergents eschew Bibleolatry.

Emergents are a *narrative* people as opposed to, say, doctrinal, dogmatic, systematic, or propositional. They love stories and gravitate toward the narrative material in both the Old and New Testaments. They are often written off as merely postevangelical postmodernists, but with respect to Scripture they differ greatly from secular postmodernists. Secular postmodernists are queasy about metanarratives; but emergents see the overarching story of God with us from Genesis to Revelation. They do not doubt God's living, active, challenging, life-altering, humbling presence in the past, present, or future; they only

seek to discern how their own story and that of their community fits in and
what that implies for their lives from this point forward. Therefore, the real
pull for them is the connection, or lack of, between their own experience and
the Bible. They do not feel compelled to smush their experience into biblical
categories. If there's a disconnect, they want to explore it and see if the "problem" has to do with the Bible or their own assumptions. One emergent has
the following as her tagline at the bottom of her e-mail: "I believe in parables.
I navigate life by using stories where I find them, and I hold tight to the ones
that tell me new kinds of truth."[11]

Emergents are *whole-Bible* people. The lectionary approach can appear
troublesome since it tends to clean things up. For emergents, the devil is in
the details, especially the troubling details.

Emergents reject *binary paradigms*. Where others see either/or, they see
both/and. Thus they do not abide a secular/sacred divide. Everything in
the universe was created by God and is loved by God. They hear the call
of the prophetic literature. Because they are heavily missional, they worry
about God's world and feel personal, global responsibility. This makes them
immerse themselves in biblical texts about the stranger and alien, the orphan
and widow, the "least of these" in our midst. The kingdom of God (or reign
of God, for those attentive to inclusive language) consumes them and convicts
them. Therefore, hospitality and charity and inclusiveness are highly valued.
Many emergents have experienced a sense of exclusion and being the odd
person out, so they are sympathetic to the plight of the misfit.

Jesus is the canon within the canon for emergents. They relate to him
and take note of the types of people he hung out with. They feel his call on
their lives and try to live out his vision. Therefore in the New Testament the
emphasis is on the Gospel stories. As one member of an emerging church
recently wrote to me: "I am now trying (on my best days) to be a living text
much like Jesus is for me. For me, I need Scripture to come alive, not just in
the reading and hearing of it because I think the Bible is filled with wonderful and horrible stories that need to be heard, but I need to struggle with it,
fight with it, love on it, be loved by it, create just worlds with it, etc" (used
by permission). Emergents are missional; they are praxis oriented; this leads
many to take political action.

Emerging churches consider the Bible to be "a member of the community"
whose voice must be heard and respected but not blindly obeyed. The Bible
is meant to open a conversation, not shut it down. I use the word "conversation" advisedly here because it's a key practice that appears in the movement.

11. Quoting Barbara Kingsolver, *Small Wonder* (New York: Harper-Collins Publishers, 2002), 6.

The worship service doesn't have a sermon: it has a "conversation."[12] In place of Sunday school, there are Adult Conversations. One could say that here emergents have been deeply influenced by postmodernism and *reader-response criticism*, wherein the text does not have meaning until the reader or reading community imbues it with such.[13]

On the other hand, we could argue that emergents model an ancient practice, a rabbinical approach to Scripture. Remember that in Jewish tradition one has both the Written Torah and the Oral Torah, both given to Moses. The Oral Torah was codified in writing around 200 CE by Judah the Prince and is called the Mishnah. The Babylonian Talmud, which modern Jews still use, was produced in the 5th century CE. Looking at the Talmud, you see a passage from the Mishnah (2nd century) in the middle of the page, along with the earliest commentary, called the Gemara (4–6th century). Around the outside is later commentary by other rabbis, including Rashi (1040–1105). The rabbis rarely agree on their interpretations. For Jews, the Talmud is the primary scriptural text, and it contains the many layers of ongoing conversation about the meaning of each passage. In other words, our Jewish brothers and sisters have *canonized conversation* and believe that God delights in ongoing process and conversation.

So, like the rabbis, emergents remain in dialogue with the tradition and see biblical interpretation as the work of each generation for its own context; the Bible is a living force to experience, not a cadaver to dissect. Interpretive certainty is elusive but certainty is not the point. Like the rabbis, emergents are passionate and confident and feel conviction about their interpretation, but not certainty. There's no need to resolve the debate, but we are constantly called to dig deeper and deeper and especially to puzzle over the, well, puzzling aspects of Scripture.

One might also find similarities between the emerging approach and the four senses of Scripture used by Catholics from the time of the church father Origen onward. A passage of Scripture is first to be interpreted *historically* (what did it mean to the original hearers? this is what is meant by the literal sense, which differs from Protestant notions of literalism); second, *allegorically* (so Moses is a type for Christ); third, *morally* (also called tropologically; this is the ethical life application for behavior); and fourth, *anagogically*, that is, in relation to heaven and afterlife and the final consummation of God's will for God's creation.

12. See, e.g., Doug Pagitt, *Preaching Re-imagined: The Role of the Sermon in Communities of Faith* (Grand Rapids: Zondervan, 2005).

13. For an introduction to reader-response criticism, see "Reader-Response Criticism," in The Bible and Culture Collective, *The Postmodern Bible* (New Haven, CT: Yale University Press, 1995), 20–69.

So, just where the emergents are accused by their BBC fellows for being most modern by steering away from the so-called literal, commonsense meaning of the Bible, that's actually where emergents are planted on very traditional ground, as viewed from many angles of their Judeo-Christian heritage! I wonder how aware BBCs are of talmudic and Catholic interpretive traditions, which certainly have a far greater claim to antiquity than modern biblicist notions, which are based on Enlightenment, Newtonian principles. We tend to think of multivalent readings as a newfangled, postmodern notion. But by their strategies, emergents show their bent for something old and something new, à la Matthew 13:52: "And he said to them, 'Therefore every scribe who has been trained for the kingdom of heaven is like the master of a household who brings out of his treasure what is new and what is old.'"

Emergents value *diversity* and *inclusivity*, which makes them *ecumenical*. Because of their epistemological humility and their knowledge of the destruction unleashed by those operating under the banner of ABSOLUTE TRUTH and strong lines of insiders/outsiders, emergents tend to show respect for other traditions. Their critics accuse them of a relativism that denies any truth, but that is an unfair accusation. Emergents believe that God is the author of all truth but that truth appears in many forms. They aren't afraid of allowing extrabiblical truth to influence their biblical interpretations. Indeed, these days it may be our scientists who are more spiritual and attuned to mystery than are many religionists. This explains why emergents, unlike their BBC compatriots, happily employ monastic disciplines in their spirituality (indeed, there is a whole neomonastic aspect to emergent Christianity). Again, their evangelical critics who are tied into modernist, scientific, analytic strategies of interpretation tend to be suspicious of these practices. Really, anything that comes from the Catholics makes most Southern Baptists squirm.

Emergent ecclesiology heavily shapes their biblical interpretation. In contrast to most forms of Christianity, it is nonhierarchical and assumes the Holy Spirit works among the gathered group to pronounce or ferret out the good news from a biblical text on any given day. Thus no one is considered to be an expert on God or to have the special prerogative of acting as God's mouthpiece. Yes, I am the New Testament expert at my church, but I'm not the God expert even though I'm ordained. Notions of authority work differently among emergents. Nothing and no one has unquestioned, prima facie, absolute authority; authority is earned and always provisional. How does this compare to your own tradition? "Figure out who has the authority to interpret Scripture in your church. That is, who will get listened to respectfully, and who won't? What do people have to do (or be) to get this status?"[14]

14. White, *Postmodernism 101*, 38.

Emergents tend to value education and be well read. It's nothing in the course of a gathering to hear names like Plato, Buber, Nietzsche, Moltmann, Caputo, Volf, Gadamer, or the postmodern giants like Lyotard, Derrida, and Foucault. They bring all of this to the biblical texts so that every angle is approached. Emergents tend to think, and this can make them high-maintenance people to pastor.

Emergents are extremely communal. They do not countenance a spirituality where it's "me, Jesus, and my Bible." They do *not* "Come to the Garden Alone." Well, maybe they do, but then they quickly text their friends or post their status on Facebook or Twitter to find out if what the Son of God disclosed was normal or concerning. This anti-lone-ranger urge is quite likely a reaction to the excesses of some BBCs' focus on salvation as an individual experience, whose main purpose is to ensure procurement of a mansion in the sky and avoid the fires of hell. Emergents certainly invite and expect individuals to do their spiritual work, whatever that may be, and they work from a notion of communal accountability, though mostly of a gentle, nonjudgmental sort. But by gentle and nonjudgmental I don't mean uninvolved. If you want insight into yourself, your emergent brothers and sisters will most likely offer observations; but they will not blow smoke since authenticity is a deep value of emergent communities. In that way, they seem to be somewhere between certain churches that busybody into your business inappropriately in a paternalistic, perhaps even cultish kind of way, and liberal churches that politely refrain from being in your business to any degree that matters for spiritual transformation.

Emergents tend to "do life together." In common parlance, you might say "they spend a lot of time together outside of church," but that would be a problematic statement on many counts. First of all, many don't meet in a physical church building at all. They rent a space here or there, or they meet in homes or in a restaurant. Second, the notion of "outside church" implies that one can move between church and life as if they are different spheres; no emergent would buy that. It's all of a piece, and one does not change one's persona, behavior, dress, speech, or conversation topics; one doesn't put on a "church face" to come to church and make the pastor and congregation believe one has it all together. Emergents are hyperlinked and extremely technology savvy, and social networks are a given. Just visit emergentvillage.com for 10 minutes and you'll understand what I mean.

This way of being church tends to draw in some unchurched people; they aren't seeking, but they come via relationships since church spreads throughout life. Many emergent churches contain the extremes: burnt Baptists and totally secular, even atheist folks. These people tend to feel welcome to contribute to the conversation during worship even as first-time visitors. So in terms of our present topic, Scripture's meaning is best discerned in *community*.

Emergents are heavy on incarnation, on embodied faith that involves all of the senses. The Bible might be acted out in surprising or poetic ways; people might be invited to draw, to make prayer beads as they reflect on what God is saying through the text, or to pull a Scripture out of a sandbox. Emergents tend to value art, and art certainly can present the biblical text in a new way. There is an emphasis on the Experiential. The Tactile. The Creative. The Artistic. There is a concern not to simply locate one's faith in one's head. But understand this: *Emergents want to be engaged, not simply entertained*; they don't need to be protected from the Bible; they don't need it watered down and made palatable; they want to talk about it as it appears. This seems different to me from "seeker-sensitive" interpretive practices.

If the Word of God became flesh and dwelt among us—that is, if the Word of God came out of the birth canal of a woman's body, grew, ate, went to the bathroom, bathed, struggled against demons, sweated, wept, exulted, was transfigured, was physically violated, and rotted away in a tomb just before being gloriously resurrected—then the Bible must have flesh on it. If a valley of dry bones can live again, then bones and blood and bread and flesh and bodies should never be left behind when we are trying to understand the grime and glory of Scripture. Any interpretation that denounces the material, created order, including our own bodies, should be suspect. From birth to death our bodies swell and shrink; they are wet with milk and sweat and urine and vomit and sex and blood and water, and wounds that fester and stink and are healed and saved and redeemed and die and are resurrected. If you can't glory in or at least talk about these basic realities in church while reading Scripture, then how can Scripture truly intersect with or impact life? We might as well just go read a Jane Austen novel—though I doubt we'll ever be transformed or made whole or saved by it.

PROMISES AND PITFALLS
OF POSTMODERN APPROACHES

Postmodern approaches remind us of the power that readers have, collectively or individually, over the text when determining its meaning. They remind us that texts cannot literally speak for themselves; they are always interpreted by readers who come from particular philosophical, epistemological, cultural locations that influence and, to some degree, predetermine the kinds of interpretive outcomes that ensue. These approaches call us to be self-aware and honest about the biases we bring to the text.

They also help us to regain a sense of imaginative play when engaging the texts; Scripture becomes a wide-open playground rife with delights to discover rather than a small dingy gray prison with solid bars that restrict us, "protect" us from ourselves, and insist that play is dangerous. Postmoderns will not settle for merely understanding what *is* and submitting to that; they do cartwheels in a field of what *may be*.

Regarding potential pitfalls of postmodernism, in its extreme forms it may sometimes "throw the baby out with the bathwater" in its critique of institutionalized Christianity. It can lead to elitism and arrogance in its rejection of what came before, as if its practitioners are somehow smarter, more honest, and more insightful than any Christians before them. Cynicism can mask ignorance. Notions of truth or authorial intention can be jettisoned to such a degree that one wonders what the point would be anyway of gathering together in a group to study and interpret a given text. Instead of the text having absolute power over the reader so as to rob the reader of the opportunity to challenge the text, now the reader has so much power over the text that the text cannot challenge or confront the reader in any worthwhile way. At their best, postmodern approaches can act prophetically to call a morally flabby church to stand up for justice and the least of these; at their worst, they become exercises in solipsistic navel-gazing.

What of the tradition do postmodern Christians hope to pass on to the children in their churches and how do they plan to do that?

STUDY QUESTIONS

1. Break into small groups and discuss the 1 Corinthians passage. Have one person in the group remain silent and observe the process. Try to note some of the assumptions about Scripture as God's address to the Christian community. What methods of interpretation do people in the group use to understand the text? What stands out and what's missing? Reconvene in a large group and debrief the process.
2. Break into small groups and discuss the Acts passage. Have one person in the group remain silent and observe the process. Try to identify some of the assumptions about Scripture as God's address to the Christian community. What methods of interpretation do people in the group use to understand the text? What stands out and what's missing? Reconvene in a large group and debrief the process.
3. What do you hope for your church and for yourself with respect to the Bible?
4. How does the Bible actually function in your church when it is gathered as a community (e.g., Sunday school for all ages; midweek gatherings; worship)?
5. Do people bring Bibles with them? Are they in the pews? Is the text projected on a screen?

6. How does the Bible function in the lives of the individuals in your church? Does anyone read it daily? Family devotionals? Never read it? Why or why not?

7. Would your people consider the Bible to be authoritative for your church or for the individuals in it? What would they mean by "authoritative"? Would they consider it sacred? What would they mean by "sacred"?

8. What aspects of modernist interpretive strategies would you say are helpful or important?

9. What aspects of postmodern interpretive strategies would you say are helpful or important?

3

Four Gospels

Problem or Gift?

Have you ever wondered why there are four different Gospels in the New Testament instead of one? In fact, having four sometimes creates confusion because certain discrepancies arise. In that case, how do we know which account is "true"? As the saying goes, "A person with one watch always knows what time it is; a person with two watches is never sure."

Take, for instance, the story about Jesus Cleansing the Temple (sometimes referred to as his "temple tantrum"). In the Synoptic Gospels (Matthew, Mark, and Luke), this event occurs at the end of Jesus' ministry and provides the final straw for Jesus' opponents, who decide he has to be killed; in John, this event occurs at the beginning of Jesus' ministry. Given these data, the reader has to decide whether (1) the Synoptics are right and John is wrong; (2) to harmonize the accounts and try to argue that the event occurred twice, once at the beginning and once at the end; or (3) there is another way to view the situation.

TO HARMONIZE OR NOT TO HARMONIZE?

Many Gospel readers automatically and unconsciously conflate and harmonize the Gospels as a way to "solve" apparent differences, contradictions, aporiae (textual seams), lacunae (gaps, omissions), additions, and so on. The practice is promoted and encouraged by the church, particularly through liturgical habits such as sermons on the Seven Last Words from the Cross. Let's briefly explore the harmonizing tendency and alternatives to it, attending at every turn to the logic and motivation behind each approach as well as what may be lost or gained by using various approaches. I will emphasize the usefulness of employing multiple approaches, whether diachronic or synchronic.[1] To do this, I will need to help readers discern for themselves why they are reading the texts anyway, what they hope to find there, if anything, and which techniques fit different aims. Ultimately, I will invite readers to allow the beauty, complexity, and, at times, mystery of the texts and the process of interpretation to reveal the beauty, complexity, and mystery of the God to whom the texts testify.

TO HARMONIZE

This is a true story. Just as I was sitting at my computer about to write this section of this chapter, I received an e-mail from A Word a Day, a site managed by Anu Garg. The entry was as follows:

maudlin

PRONUNCIATION: (MAWD-lin)

MEANING: *adjective:* Overly sentimental.

ETYMOLOGY: After Mary Magdalene, a Biblical character who was a follower of Jesus. In medieval art she was depicted as a penitent weeping for her sins (she washed the feet of Jesus with her tears) and her name became synonymous with tearful sentimentality.
    The name Magdalene means "of Magdala" in Greek and is derived after a town on the Sea of Galilee. The name Magdala, in turn, means "tower" in Aramaic. So here we have a word coined after a person, who was named after a place, which was named after a thing.
    In an allusion to her earlier life, Mary Magdalene's name has sprouted another eponym, magdalene, meaning a reformed prostitute.[2]

This is a perfect example of the problem of harmonizing: conflating different stories from the various Gospels to create a single story, though that single invented story does not appear whatsoever in the New Testament. But don't take my word for it.

---

1. *Diachronic* refers to approaches that study the development of a text over time, from Greek *dia-* (through) + *chronos-* (time), from the oral stages through the commitment to writing and editing. *Synchronic* refers to approaches that attend to the final form of text without regard for its historical development over time.
    2. http://wordsmith.org/words/maudlin.html.

The Facts about Mary Magdalene
(According to the Bible)[3]

Mary Magdalene in Matthew

Mary Magdalene appears first (canonically speaking) in Matthew 27:55–56, along with another Mary and another woman watching the crucifixion: "Many women were also there, looking on from a distance; they had followed Jesus from Galilee and had provided for him. Among them were Mary Magdalene, and Mary the mother of James and Joseph, and the mother of the sons of Zebedee." She appears next with "the other Mary" in 27:61, "sitting opposite the tomb." Finally, she and "the other Mary" go to the tomb on Easter: "After the sabbath, as the first day of the week was dawning, Mary Magdalene and the other Mary went to see the tomb" (28:1).

Mary Magdalene in Mark

In Mark, as in Matthew, Mary Magdalene appears only at the crucifixion and tomb:

> There were also women looking on from a distance; among them were Mary Magdalene, and Mary the mother of James the younger and of Joses, and Salome. (15:40)
> Mary Magdalene and Mary the mother of Joses saw where the body was laid. (15:47)
> When the sabbath was over, Mary Magdalene, and Mary the mother of James, and Salome bought spices, so that they might go and anoint him. (16:1)
> Now after he rose early on the first day of the week, he appeared first to Mary Magdalene, from whom he had cast out seven demons. (16:9)

Mary Magdalene in Luke

In Luke, Mary Magdalene first appears during Jesus' ministry along with the disciples and some other important women:

> Soon afterwards he went on through cities and villages, proclaiming and bringing the good news of the kingdom of God. The twelve were with him, as well as some women who had been cured of evil spirits and infirmities: Mary, called Magdalene, from whom seven demons had gone out, and Joanna, the wife of Herod's steward Chuza, and Susanna, and many others, who provided for them out of their resources. (8:1–3)

---

3 See also Jaime Clark-Soles, "Introducing the Real Mary Magdalene." No pages. http://sbl-site.org/educational/TBnewsletter.aspx.

In narrating Easter morning, Luke speaks of unnamed women who go to the tomb, find Jesus risen, and go back to proclaim the gospel to the disciples. At that point Luke names them: "Now it was Mary Magdalene, Joanna, Mary the mother of James, and the other women with them who told this to the apostles" (24:10).

Mary Magdalene in John[4]

Finally, Mary Magdalene appears in a crucial role in the Gospel of John. In John, Mary Magdalene is standing right at the foot of the cross and witnesses the birth of the church as Jesus gives his mother and beloved disciple to one another: "Meanwhile, standing near the cross of Jesus were his mother, and his mother's sister, Mary the wife of Clopas, and Mary Magdalene. When Jesus saw his mother and the disciple whom he loved standing beside her, he said to his mother, 'Woman, here is your son.' Then he said to the disciple, 'Here is your mother.' And from that hour the disciple took her into his own home" (19:25–27).

As if that were not a powerful enough scene, Mary Magdalene becomes the first to encounter the risen Lord by herself and the first preacher of the resurrection in Christian history, according to John. It is *she* who proclaims the resurrection of Jesus to the disciples.

> Early on the first day of the week, while it was still dark, Mary Mag-dalene came to the tomb and saw that the stone had been removed from the tomb. (20:1)
>
> But Mary stood weeping outside the tomb. As she wept, she bent over to look into the tomb; and she saw two angels in white, sitting where the body of Jesus had been lying, one at the head and the other at the feet. They said to her, "Woman, why are you weeping?" She said to them, "They have taken away my Lord, and I do not know where they have laid him." When she had said this, she turned around and saw Jesus standing there, but she did not know that it was Jesus. Jesus said to her, "Woman, why are you weeping? Whom are you looking for?" Supposing him to be the gardener, she said to him, "Sir, if you have carried him away, tell me where you have laid him, and I will take him away." Jesus said to her, "Mary!" She turned and said to him in Hebrew, "Rabbouni!" (which means Teacher). Jesus said to her, "Do not hold on to me, because I have not yet ascended to the Father. But go to my brothers and say to them, 'I am ascending to my Father and your Father, to my God and your God.'" Mary Magdalene went and announced to the disciples, "I have seen the Lord"; and she told them that he had said these things to her. (20:11–18)

4. For visual images of Mary Magdalene in John, see http://catholic-resources.org/John/Art20.html.

Mary Magdalene: An Anointing Prostitute? NOT!

You the reader have just read all of the passages in the Bible that refer to Mary Magdalene. Where do you find in these texts any mention of her anointing Jesus' feet or being a prostitute? You don't. Then why is it that if you walk up to most Christians and say, "Quick. Tell me everything you know about Mary Magdalene," you will likely hear all about her prostitute ways and her anointing act (which never appears in Scripture), but nothing about Scripture's testimony to her role in supporting Jesus' ministry (Luke 8), her faithful appearance at the cross, her witness to the resurrection, her role as an apostle (defined as someone who walked with Jesus and was sent to proclaim the good news of his resurrection), and John's designation of her as the first preacher in Christian history?[5]

Harmonization leads to harlotization. The urge to simplify and reduce to a lowest common denominator has led to combining the various anointing stories on the one hand and some of the Marys on the other. Let's sort them out so that we get clear on what the Bible *actually* says versus what interpreters of the Bible have *said* that it says.

The Anointings

Anointing in Matthew

In Matthew 26:6–13, Jesus is in Bethany at the home of Simon the leper:

> Now while Jesus was at Bethany in the house of Simon the leper, a woman came to him with an alabaster jar of very costly ointment, and she poured it on his *head* as he sat at the table. But when the disciples saw it, they were angry and said, "Why this waste? For this ointment could have been sold for a large sum, and the money given to the poor." But Jesus, aware of this, said to them, "Why do you trouble the woman? She has performed a good service for me. For you always have the poor with you, but you will not always have me. By pouring this ointment on my body she has prepared me for burial. Truly I tell you, wherever this good news is proclaimed in the whole world, what she has done will be told in remembrance of her."

An unnamed woman appears and anoints Jesus' *head* (not his feet). The woman is not a prostitute, not a sinner, and is not named Mary. There are no tears and she needs no forgiveness. She has served Jesus; he has not served her.

---

5. For a provocative, scholarly treatment of Mary Magdalene, see Jane Schaberg with Melanie Johnson-DeBaufre, *Mary Magdalene Understood* (New York: Continuum, 2006).

Anointing in Mark

In Mark 14:3–10, as in Matthew, Simon is identified as a leper. An unnamed woman appears and anoints *Jesus' head*. In Matthew, it's the disciples who chastise the woman. Not so in Mark. John, on the other hand, singles out Judas Iscariot as the culprit. Again, observe that the woman is not a prostitute, not a sinner, and is not named Mary. There are no tears and she needs no forgiveness. She has served Jesus; he has not served her.

Anointing in Luke

In Luke 7:37–50 the anointing occurs at the home of a man named Simon, as in Matthew and Mark, but this Simon is a Pharisee, not a leper. There is no mention of Bethany (the last city mentioned is Nain). An unnamed woman who is labeled a "sinner" (not a prostitute) entered and "stood behind him at his *feet*, weeping, and began to bathe his feet with her tears and to dry them with her hair. Then she continued kissing his feet and anointing them with the ointment." Simon is offended so Jesus tells a story that indicts Simon, but Jesus extends forgiveness to the woman, saying that her faith has "saved" her. Unlike in Matthew, Mark, and John, this act is not a service to Jesus that foreshadows his death. It is placed far earlier in Jesus' ministry, and Luke does not tie it to the Passion. This story has obviously been erroneously imposed upon Mary Magdalene and has given rise to the notion of her as a tearful penitent, a reformed "bad girl of the Bible."

Anointing in John

In John 12 Jesus is in Bethany, the town where the siblings Mary, Martha, and the resuscitated Lazarus reside.

> Mary took a pound of costly perfume made of pure nard, anointed Jesus' *feet*, and wiped them with her hair. The house was filled with the fragrance of the perfume. But Judas Iscariot, one of his disciples (the one who was about to betray him), said, "Why was this perfume not sold for three hundred denarii and the money given to the poor?" (He said this not because he cared about the poor, but because he was a thief; he kept the common purse and used to steal what was put into it.) Jesus said, "Leave her alone. She bought it so that she might keep it for the day of my burial. You always have the poor with you, but you do not always have me." (12:3–8)

This Mary is not a "sinner" and is not Magdalene. Like the woman in Luke, she anoints Jesus' feet and uses her hair, but there are no tears and it has nothing to do with repentance. As in Matthew and Mark, the anointing woman is shown as understanding who Jesus is and what fate soon awaits him in a way the disciples do not. In Matthew and Mark, the woman is scolded by multiple detractors; in John, that role falls upon Judas Iscariot alone.

The Named Marys

Good luck, reader, sorting out all the Marys!

Marys in Matthew

At least two Marys appear in Matthew: Mary, Jesus' mother (who appears by name[6] at 1:16, 18, 20; 2:11; and 13:55), and Mary Magdalene (who appears at 27:56, 61; and 28:1). In Matthew 27:56 we read: "Among them were Mary Magdalene, and Mary the mother of James and Joseph, and the mother of the sons of Zebedee." There are at least two women here, probably three. In Mark, Mary, Jesus' mother, is named as the mother of James and Joses (Joseph), so it's not unreasonable to assume that this Mary in Matthew 27 is Jesus' mother. The mother of the sons of Zebedee is presumably a third woman. Matthew 27:61 and 28:1 refer to "the other Mary." The only other Mary consistently presented in Matthew and Mark is Jesus' mother, so it may be a reference to her. If not, it's a third, mysterious Mary.

Marys in Mark

Mark has two Marys: Jesus' mother and Mary Magdalene. Jesus' mother first appears by name at 6:3:[7] "Is not this the carpenter, the son of Mary [that makes her Jesus' mother] and brother of James and Joses and Judas and Simon, and are not his sisters here with us?" Here Mary is the mother of Jesus, James, Joses, Judas, Simon, and multiple daughters. So when Mark refers in 15:40 to "Mary the mother of James the younger and of Joses," it may indicate Jesus' mother. Same thing in Mark 15:47 where we hear of Mary, the mother of Joses. I assume that's the same Mary that the author refers to in 6:3 and 15:40 as the author ties this Mary to Joses. In 16:1 the author refers to Mary the mother of James; again, perhaps this refers to the Mary first mentioned in 6:3 and then 15:40, Jesus' mother. Mary Magdalene appears at 15:40, 47; 16:1 (and 16:9 if you're an advocate of the longer ending).

Marys in Luke

In addition to Jesus' mother (Luke 1:27, 30, 34, 38, 39, 46, 56; 2:5, 16, 19, 34) and Magdalene (8:2; 24:10), Luke includes Mary, the sister of Martha (10:39,

---

6. She appears unnamed at Matthew 12:46–47, but here we are interested only in the appearances of the name Mary.

7. She appears unnamed at Mark 3:31–32, but here we are interested only in the appearances of the name Mary.

42). In that story, remember, Martha is engaged in domestic duties while Mary "has chosen the better part" by sitting at Jesus' feet and listening (she does *not* anoint said feet; also there is no mention that Mary and Martha have a brother Lazarus at all). Luke 24:10 speaks of Mary the mother of James, which, as indicated by Mark and Matthew, probably means Jesus' mother. If it's not Jesus' mother, there's a mysterious Mary. So there are at least three Marys in Luke: Jesus' mother, Mary Magdalene, and the Mary who is Martha's sister. None is a prostitute, sinner, or anointer.

Marys in John

John names three Marys: Mary, the sister of Lazarus and Martha (11:1, 2, 19, 20, 28, 31, 32, 45; 12:3); Mary Magdalene (19:25; 20:1, 11, 16, 18); and Mary, the wife of Clopas (19:25). Though Jesus' mother appears in the Gospel, John never names her.

By reviewing the data, we find that there is *no* Mary who is a prostitute, and the only Mary who anoints is not Magdalene but Martha's sister and only in John. The harmonizing tendency has created a character who never actually appears in Scripture! In 591 that harmonization was made official by Pope Gregory the Great, who declared: "She whom Luke calls the sinful woman, whom John calls Mary [of Bethany], we believe to be the Mary from whom seven devils were ejected according to Mark."[8] Our poor 6th-century ancestors had no way to fight back, however, since they did not have access to the Bible (or much education) except through church officials. We, on the other hand, have no excuse for tolerating gross misrepresentations of the details of the biblical texts. Shame on Pope Gregory.

One might work through all of this and throw up one's hands and say, "It's too hard to keep all this straight. Who cares?" I would argue that Scripture matters enough to do the work of keeping it straight. I would also argue that laziness should not be a warrant for rewriting Scripture. If one is going to rewrite Scripture by simplifying it, why stop there? Why not just scrap the text altogether and write a new, simpler story that one finds easier to deal with and "keep straight"? In other words, making such a move indicates that one does not actually consider the texts authoritative; they cease to be Scripture. The harlotization of Mary Magdalene (not to mention the Samaritan woman of John 4) has done damage to Mary Magdalene and the legacy the authors intended for her and has, at the very least, contributed to the church's ongoing negative view of women, their leadership in the church, and the nature of female sexuality.

8. Pope Gregory the Great, in a sermon on September 21, 591: *Homily 33*, in Patrologia latina (PL) 76, col. 1239; reported at http://www.catholic.net/index.php?size=mas&id=2886& option=dedestaca.

Seven Last Words from the Cross

I wonder if the church's Holy Week practice of preaching on Jesus' so-called "Seven Last Words from the Cross" perpetuates a harmonizing tendency among Christians.

No one Gospel depicts Jesus as saying all of these seven sentences; the list can be created only by combining all four Gospels into one long story, filling in the "gaps" in one Gospel with caulk from the other Gospels. Harmonizing. What is gained and what is lost by such a move? One might argue that this tradition is less problematic than that of Mary Magdalene insofar as the words ascribed to Jesus actually appear somewhere in the Bible itself. Certainly reflecting upon the cross during Lent is a desirable Christian practice; but the Seven Last Words tradition may tempt us to do so at the expense of each Gospel's particularity.[9]

It would be far better to consider Jesus' passion in each Gospel separately; in fact, not doing so gives the impression of a very confused, moody, erratic Jesus on the cross. The way each Gospel writer tells the story of the passion is tied to the way each has presented Jesus before the passion. Each Gospel is a self-contained piece of literature and should be read on its own terms first so that the reader understands the major themes and techniques and convictions of the evangelists. Once that's done, one can fruitfully compare the Gospels, note the similarities and differences, and then ponder the significance of those differences for the original hearers as well as for our own theologies today.

The Seven Last Words

1. "Father, forgive them; for they do not know what they are doing" (Luke 23:34).
2. "Truly, I say to you, today you will be with me in Paradise" (Luke 23:43).
3. "When Jesus saw his mother and the disciple whom he loved standing beside her, he said to his mother, 'Woman, here is your son.' Then he said to the disciple, 'Here is your mother'" (John 19:26–27).
4. "Eli, Eli, lama sabachthani?" that is, "My God, my God, why have you forsaken me?" (Matt. 27:46).
5. "I am thirsty" (John 19:28).
6. "It is finished" (John 19:30).
7. "Father, into your hands I commend my spirit" (Luke 23:46).

9. Granted, if each of the seven words from the cross is treated in an entirely different service with different music and different speakers, harmonizing may be less likely. Maybe.

In Matthew and Mark, for instance, Jesus utters his cry of dereliction. But any serious student of the Fourth Gospel knows that John would never depict Jesus as crying out, "My God, my God, why have you forsaken me," since in John, Jesus is equal to God and, in fact, participated in creation. As such, Jesus knows everything (John 2:24–25), and he confidently and fluidly unfolds the plan for what John calls Jesus' glorification and exaltation on the cross. When the work that he came to do is complete, Jesus says so: "It is finished" (John 19:30). Again, it would not make sense for John's Jesus to say, "Father into your hands I commend my spirit" for a number of reasons. First, Jesus repeatedly notes in John that "I and the Father are one." Second, the Spirit in John (and only in John) is called the Paraclete (Advocate, Comforter) and is bestowed upon Jesus' followers at the time of his death.

Jesus is quite reticent in Mark; notice that he makes only that one poignant statement from the cross, a bereft cry. Mark's Jesus could never say, "Woman, here is your son. . . . Here is your mother," as he does in John because Mark made it clear in chapter 14 that Jesus had been utterly deserted by his followers (14:50); some women looked on, but only "from a distance" (Mark 15:40). On the other hand, Jesus is quite talkative from the cross in both Luke and John. Anything he says in Luke he says only in Luke; likewise with John.

To harmonize the Seven Last Words profoundly affects the work of Christology, that is, the area of Christian doctrine devoted to the nature of Jesus the Christ and his work. When we mesh all of the distinct Gospel narratives, we create a Jesus that none of the evangelists' own original audiences would have recognized since they did not have access to four different Gospels placed side by side as we do. Blessing or curse?

NOT TO HARMONIZE

From the 2nd century onward, certain people have tried to remedy the "problem" of four Gospels, which are not identical, by producing a harmony of the four Gospels in which the details of each Gospel are taken and fitted into a single overarching narrative so as to eliminate any apparent contradictions. Most famously, Tatian's *Diatessaron* was constructed in Syria in the 2nd century and continued to function authoritatively there until the 5th century.[10] Irenaeus, a 2nd-century bishop in what is now Lyons, France, was the first

---

10. *The Jefferson Bible*, or, *The Life and Morals of Jesus of Nazareth*, created by Thomas Jefferson (ca. 1820; published, Washington, DC: National Museum, 1885), follows some of the same tendencies, but it has other aims besides a thorough unified chronological rendering of all the Gospel data: http://www.beliefnet.com/resourcelib/docs/62/The_Jefferson_Bible_The_Life_Morals_of_Jesus_of_Nazareth_1.html.

"But it is not possible that the Gospels can be either more or fewer in number than they are. For since there are four zones of the world in which we live, and four principal winds, while the church has been scattered throughout the world, and since the 'pillar and ground' of the Church is the Gospel and the spirit of life, it is fitting that she should have four pillars, breathing incorruption on every side, and vivifying human afresh. From this fact, it is evident that the Logos, the fashioner [*demiourgos*] of all, he that sits on the cherubim and holds all things together, when he was manifested to humanity, gave us the gospel under four forms but bound together by one spirit." (Irenaeus, *Against Heresies* 3.11.8.)

to argue in favor of four Gospels. Perhaps he did so in reaction to Tatian's *Diatessaron*, to Marcion's insistence that only the Gospel of Luke should be used, and to the gnostic dependence upon John alone, and so on. In the 4th century, the Christian canon was defined, and we have had four canonical Gospels since then. The church, then, canonized diversity from the start. Presumably the church could have canonized Tatian's *Diatessaron* or some other harmony and therefore made it such that later Christians would not have to deal with inconsistencies. But we have been given (gifted with) four Gospels, not one; Scripture is revelatory literature that has the power to transform. But the texts can't reveal if we don't allow them to speak, if we try to smooth over inconsistencies and puzzles and pretend they aren't there. Perhaps if we revel in them, they will reveal. If we suppress them, they can't surprise us.

QUESTIONS OF GENRE

What kind of literature is a Gospel anyway? Clearly it's a narrative, but what kind of narrative? Is it most like a historical account? If so, from whose perspective—first person or third person? Is it more like historical fiction? It should be obvious that the Gospels do not approximate a news report. Is it like an ancient novel? Notice that in each Gospel the narrator writes from an omniscient perspective. He or she can tell us what a character is thinking in their head but never says out loud. He can tell us what is transpiring in the praetorium between Jesus and Pilate (John 18:33) while also training our eyes on Peter's encounter outside the gates (18:16). Obviously a finite person cannot have actual access to all of this information simultaneously. The authors of the Gospels have created a narrative, and the Gospels follow literary conventions.

They make heavy use of symbolism (I am the Vine; I am the Good Shepherd; my flesh is true food, my blood is true drink); allegory (see the story of the King Who Gave a Great Banquet in Matt. 22); parables and other figures of speech (the kingdom of heaven is like a mustard seed . . .); and hyberbole (if your eye causes you to sin, pluck it out). Jesus loves to tell stories to make his point. Take the parables of the Good Samaritan and the Prodigal Son. When Jesus tells these stories, he's not entertaining his audience with a recounting of something historical that he has witnessed; he's conveying truth by means of story. The characters don't have to be historical, and the action doesn't have to conform to every literal historical constraint of its period to be "true." Read good fiction and poetry, and you'll know what I mean.

Story?

Truth, Belief, Reality, and History. For many courses that I teach, I assign the incisive chapters from Dostoyevsky's *The Brothers Karamazov* titled "Rebellion" and "The Legend of the Grand Inquisitor." Is the Legend of the Grand Inquisitor "true"? Well, what do you mean by true—that it happened in some point in history and was properly recorded and notarized? No. Is it true? Of course. Is Ivan "real"? Should we conduct a Quest for the historical Ivan? Must we dig behind the text to discover whether Dostoyevsky knew a historical man named Ivan Karamazov? Do we have to discern which part of Ivan, if any, is really a projection of Dostoyevsky's own personality and then discard Dostoyevsky's influence, or can we simply read Ivan as "real" just as he stands in the text—conveying shattering truths about the human situation? Is fiction "true"? Are the biblical stories "true"?

In connection with this question, which always comes up with respect to the Gospels, I show a clip from the movie *Secondhand Lions*. Robert Duvall plays Uncle Hub, who has told his young nephew, Walter, many stories about his heroic, fairy-tale-like adventures in his younger days, part of which involves falling in love with a beautiful princess named Jasmine. But Jasmine died in childbirth, along with her baby. Heartbroken, Hub went back to the Foreign Legion and fought for another 40 years, alone. One night Walter challenges the truth of these tales. Hub responds with an eloquent, provocative speech about the relationship between belief and truth: "Just because somethin' isn't true, that's no reason you can't believe in it." He goes on to explain that we are best shaped by believing in certain ideals whether they are true or not: that true love never dies, that honor outweighs power or money, and that good will eventually win over evil.

For some Christians—and you, dear reader, may be one—it is the power of stories that is important, not notions of how closely a particular recounting aligns with "what really happened" (as if any human being could actually give an unbiased, uninterpreted account of any particular historical event). For them, even if someone could prove that the Prodigal Son event never happened historically, it would not make the story less true since, most likely, they've experienced that story in their own lives or the lives of those close to them. Read John 9. Historically speaking, I don't know whether that blind guy ever existed, but I do know that that story happens every day around the world. Every day some people look at those suffering from a particular illness and ask, in their own way, "Who sinned that this man was born blind?" And every day Jesus tries to set the record straight by reforming the theology of those who would ask such a question while simultaneously healing the one born blind. And those who have found their lives healed in some way by Jesus embrace the gift and then courageously follow Jesus, even though they must endure the wrath and hatred and condescension of the religious know-it-alls in their churches or workplaces or homes. And every day they rest in their knowledge that though they were blind, now they see. And with that, they step out on faith, praising God. That's true.

Recently I taught John at a weekend preaching/lecture series. After discussing John 9 a quiet, unobtrusive woman who had faithfully come to the lectures and worship services, accompanied by her daughter who has Down Syndrome, came up to me with tears in her eyes and said, "So, you're saying it's *not* my fault that my daughter has Down Syndrome because I had her too late?" (That is, indeed, the point that I had made, but only because the text made the point first.) I was so moved by her courage, perseverance, and faith and simultaneously so angry that any Christian would burden this poor woman even further by their nescience. Stories are powerful, whether they "actually happened" or not.

History?

Other Christians find talk of myth and symbol and allegory uninteresting at best, dangerous at worst. For them, the truth of the Gospels must be grounded in historical fact(s). Probably most Christians would agree that some aspects of historicity are important to their faith. Once I asked a group of Christians whether or not it matters that the Gospels are historical in some sense. One man strongly answered yes, and I asked, "What percent would have to be true for it to count?" He replied, only half-jokingly, "87%." Christianity is a faith tradition grounded in the conviction that God acts in history—always has, always will. God gets involved in the grimy and glorious details of human life in every epoch in very particular ways with very particular people (usually very unlikely types) with astonishing results. Including each of us. Christianity is a wonderful, if perplexing, exercise in considering the importance of story and history and how the two relate.

If you want to determine your own comfort zone in this area, ask yourself: "What features of the Gospels *must* be historically accurate for my faith to stand?" The resurrection? The Virgin Birth? Herod's Slaughter of the Innocents? Jesus' birth year? Jesus' death day? The Last Supper as told by John? The Last Supper as related by the Synoptics? Jesus' words from the cross in Mark? Luke? John? All of them? Then ask yourself, Why these and not others? Why are they absolutely essential to your faith? What would be lost if the story were proved to be unhistorical?

An Exercise: *Big Fish*

Sometimes it's useful to explore these important ideas using a less emotionally charged text than one's Scriptures. The text can be written or visual. I recommend, then, that you watch the movie *Big Fish* alone or in a group and consider some of the questions provided below. At the very least, the movie *Big Fish* gets at the issues of

- the relationship between story/fact/truth
- the nature of communities that share well-known, oft-repeated (even if embellished) stories
- the ability and need to *find* the symbolic in the mundane or to *create* the symbolic from the mundane

On the day of Will Bloom's wedding, his father, Edward, steals the show by once again telling the epic tale of why he wasn't present at his son's birth: using his wedding ring, he was out catching a giant legendary fish. Will has had enough of this story, and in fact all of Edward's tall tales; he's tired of the fact that his dad is long on stories and short on facts. Will longs to know his father in a real way, but his investigative questions are always met with another (hardly believable) tale. Will loses faith and respect for his father and concludes that he cannot trust or know his father. Frustrated, Will ceases relationship and communication with his father for three years.

When his father has a stroke and is hospitalized, Will returns to Alabama from Paris with his pregnant wife, Josephine. In a series of flashbacks, we see Edward's life through his tales, a life peopled with mythic figures. There's the witch with the glass eye who tells him his future, including his death; there's the giant Karl, with whom he braves a haunted forest only to arrive at the small town of Spectre, wherein live an assortment of interesting characters. It's an idyllic town that houses the missing poet Norther Winslow and a young girl named Jenny to whom Edward becomes attached; he leaves Spectre but promises Jenny he will return. He and Karl go to work for the circus, and there Edward spots the love of his life. He works three years for Amos Calloway: Calloway gives Edward one clue a month about the girl whom Edward admires. After three years he learns her name is Sandra Templeton and she studies at Auburn University. Edward then wins Sandra by collecting all the daffodils (her favorite flower) from five states and enduring violent treatment at the hands of her current beau. He marries Sandra but is sent to the Korean War, where he meets Siamese twins Ping and Jing, who help him make it back to the United States, where he promises to make them stars. Meanwhile, Sandra has received word that he's dead so she's surprised upon his return. He becomes a traveling salesman and helps former poet Norther Winslow rob a bank and become a millionaire. Winslow gives Edward $10,000 and Edward buys Sandra's dream house.

Questions to consider:

1. Are Edward Bloom's stories true or false? Is this a good question? Why, or why not?
2. Will, the son, is always trying to dig through the stories to get to the historical Ed. How would one get to the historical Ed? What criteria would you use? What would be the point?
3. Are the stories in the Gospels true or false? Is this a good question? Why, or why not?
4. Some people search through the Gospels to get to the historical Jesus. How would one do that? What criteria would you use? What's the point of such a project?
5. Think about Scripture in relation to the movie's statement at the end that we can become the stories. Short story author Tobias Wolff writes: "That sense of kinship is what makes stories important to us. The pleasure we take in cleverness and technical virtuosity soon exhausts itself in the absence of any recognizable human landscape. We need to feel ourselves acted upon by a story, outraged, exposed, in danger of heartbreak and change. Those are the stories that endure in our memories, to the point where they take on the nature of memory itself. In this way the experience of something read can form us no less than the experience of something lived through."[*] What does this mean for those of us who have a body of scriptural texts?
6. What do you make of the scene in which Will, ever the literalist, perhaps a slave to facts, turns to story in the moment of crisis (his dad's final moments)? What could that mean for us?

[*]Tobias Wolff, ed., *The Vintage Book of American Short Stories* (New York: Vintage Contemporaries, 1994), xiii.

Will is still impatient with all these stories and aims to discover the truth of his father's life. Rifling through Edward's office, Will finds a letter from Spectre and decides to go there. He arrives at the house of Jennifer Hill, whom he suspects was his father's mistress. As it turns out, Edward was the town's savior; when Spectre went bankrupt, Edward bought it and had it restored, with the help of his friends. Though Jenny loved Edward, he remained true to Sandra. He didn't have an affair with Jenny; he saved her home and the life she loved.

Will goes to visit his father in the hospital and finds that Edward is only partly conscious and cannot speak much. His health is clearly failing. He asks Will to tell him a story of how it all ends. Clumsily but poignantly, Will learns how to tell a story, and one that matters. He narrates Edward's death; no, he narrates Edward *into* his death. In Will's story, they escape from the hospital and make their way to the river where the big fish who swallowed Edward's wedding ring lives. All of the larger-than-life figures who have populated Edward's stories appear in the story to greet Edward on this final journey. Will carries his father into the river, where Edward becomes a big fish. As Will finishes the story, his father exclaims, "Exactly!" and passes away. At the funeral Will meets the characters he's heard about so many times. As it turns out, Karl isn't really a giant, just a large man. Ping and Jing aren't conjoined; they're just twins who are from Siam. When Will's own son is born, Will passes on the stories, stating that his father *became* his stories and thereby achieved a kind of immortality.

BOTH/AND/AND/AND:
FOUR SENSES OF SCRIPTURE

Sometimes readers reduce the differences among the four Gospels to a game of textual telephone. Remember that game you played while sitting in a circle? The first person whispers a few sentences in the ear of the person next to her; then to the best of her abilities, that person relays the message to the person sitting next to her, and so on until, when the last person receives the message, he says it out loud. Usually during the transmission process the message undergoes considerable change, often to the point of being unrecognizable to the originator.

Another analogy I often encounter among people who don't quite know what to do with the variety among the Gospels is that of reporting the details of a car wreck. When asking four different people to report what they saw and how they interpreted what they saw, one will receive four different accounts that do not mesh. Everyone views events through a particular lens that makes them notice some details while missing others; each person brings background experience that may bias their own telling of the story. Perhaps they recently caused a wreck or were the victim of a wreck; this may influence their interpretation of the "facts."

But the Gospels aren't a telephone game or a car wreck. To analogize them as such demeans the intention and care that went into their creation. These are texts that have shaped and transformed lives for thousands of years, not a silly game or momentary dip into a common occurrence.

Unlike Protestant Christians, Jews and Catholics have not been as locked into a single literal historical reading of Scripture. The rabbis are famous for wrangling with one another and even with God over the ambiguities in Scripture. They never deny those contradictions or ambiguities; rather, ambiguity simply gives cause for further study, conversation, and debate. For example, take this passage:

> Rabbi Eliezer and some other rabbis were having a dispute over whether a certain oven was clean or unclean according to Scripture: "On that day R. Eliezer brought forward every imaginable argument, but they did not accept them. Said he to them: 'If halakhah (i.e., the laws of Scripture), agrees with me, let this carob-tree prove it!' Thereupon the carob-tree was torn a hundred cubits out of its place— others affirm, four hundred cubits. 'No proof can be brought from a carob-tree,' they retorted. Again he said to them: 'If the halakhah agrees with me, let the stream of water prove it!' Whereupon the stream of water flowed backwards. 'No proof can be brought from a stream of water,' they rejoined. Again he urged, 'If the halakhah agrees with me, let the walls of the schoolhouse prove it,' whereupon the walls inclined to fall. But R. Joshua rebuked them, saying: 'When scholars are engaged in a halakhic dispute, what have ye to interfere?' Hence they did not fall, in honour of R. Joshua, nor did they resume the upright, in honor of R. Eliezer; and they are still standing thus inclined. Again he said to them, 'If the halakhah agrees with me, let it be proved from Heaven!' Whereupon a Heavenly Voice cried out: 'Why do ye dispute with R. Eliezer, seeing that in all matters the halakhah agrees with him!' But R. Joshua arose and exclaimed: 'It is not in heaven.' What did he mean by this? Said R. Jeremiah: 'That the Torah had already been given at Mount Sinai; we pay no attention to a Heavenly Voice, because thou has long since written in the Torah at Mount Sinai, "After the majority one must incline."' R. Nathan met Elijah and asked him, 'What did the Holy One, blessed be He, do in that hour?' He laughed with joy, he replied, saying, 'My children have defeated Me, my children have defeated Me.'"[11]

This rabbinic story presents Scripture as a playground, not a prison. God invites us into a wide-open play space of discovery rather than slapping a

---

11. Babylonian Talmud, tractate *Baba Metzi'a* 59b.

straitjacket on us and placing us in lockdown. God takes sheer delight in our serious study of Scripture, a knowledge of it so intent that we can engage God in debate and can wrangle and wrestle with God as Jacob did at the river Jabbok (Gen. 32:21–32).

Some early Catholics adopted the rabbinic attitude of delight in the multivalence and polysemy of Scriptural texts. This is especially highlighted in the traditional Catholic system of interpretation known as the four senses of Scripture. The first sense is the literal (also called historical): the meaning intended by the original author in the original historical context.

The second sense is allegorical (including typological readings) and is often employed when inconsistencies, obscurities, or other problems arise in interpreting a text. The allegorical interpreter appeals to a deeper meaning in the text, or one that is beyond the literal, often in order to make a particular text relevant to modern Christians who might otherwise read the story as a mere historical account, far removed from their own lived experience and faith. So when the Twin Towers in New York were smashed to bits on September 11, 2001, I received a phone call from a newspaper asking me to comment on how that event related to the book of Revelation. In this approach, numbers, characters, and events in the Bible stand for something else in the interpreter's own time period. Thus Saddam Hussein became the antichrist of Revelation for the moment, and so on. The Israelites' crossing through the Red Sea is taken to refer to Christian baptism. There are better and worse allegorical interpretations. Take a look at 1 Corinthians 10:1–4 or 1 Peter 3:20–21 and see what you think.

The third sense is called tropological: it relates to the moral example of a text. The fourth sense is anagogical and has an eschatological, future focus regarding the heavenly destiny of Christians. Often those who would explain these four senses of Scripture to the uninitiated, drawing upon John Cassian, use the city of Jerusalem to exemplify how the senses function: "The one Jerusalem can be understood in four different ways, in the historical sense as the city of the Jews, in allegory as the Church of Christ, in anagoge as the heavenly city of God, 'which is the mother of us all' (Gal 4:26), in the tropological sense as the human soul."[12]

What began with the Jews and the Catholics was contested by the Reformation and Enlightenment. Here we were taught that reason and science and *only* reason and science would lead us to truth. To be "true," something had

---

12. John Cassian, *Conferences*, trans. Colm Luibheid (New York: Paulist Press, 1985), 160. For a useful article on the multiple senses of Scripture, see Sandra M. Schneiders, "Senses of Scripture," in *The HarperCollins Encyclopedia of Catholicism*, ed. Richard P. McBrien (New York: HarperCollins, 1995), 1175–76.

to be historically accurate and scientifically tenable. As I indicated in chapter 2 with postmodernist concerns, such notions have been hotly contested.

Why have I employed these examples from Jewish and Catholic exegesis? Because I want to suggest that we need not fear looking too closely at the details of the four Gospels even though doing so raises serious historical questions. But earlier interpreters did not consider this devastating to the faith and necessary to wish away or sweep under the rug or pull a Wizard of Oz outlook: "Pay no attention to the man behind the curtain." They reveled in the details and enigmas of the texts and allowed the puzzles not to scare them away from their faith but drive them deeper into it. Perhaps we can do the same.

Many people find their first deep encounter with the variety among the canonical Gospels (not to mention the noncanonical gospels) disturbing. They find their notions of the inspired authority of Scripture challenged. The same holds true of *form criticism* and *redaction criticism* (treated in the next chapter), both of which posit development of the traditions over time rather than receipt of Holy Writ straight from God's hands with no significant human participation. It is useful for a Christian to reflect upon her notions of scriptural authority. Do you consider Scripture to be an authoritative source for your life of faith? In what way? If you don't, why not? If you do, is it the primary authority or is it one among others? What might those others be? For instance, a number of traditions explicitly value reason, experience, and community along with Scripture as resources for Christian living.

God has canonized diversity and we should all take that fact personally. God has validated different ways of viewing Jesus. There's Mark's Jesus for the politically persecuted and suffering and Luke's Jesus to afflict those of us who have grown too comfortable with the status quo, who propagate the status quo, and who, God forbid, use the name of God to affirm the status quo. There's Matthew's Jesus to remind us that following Jesus means being a church and there's John's Jesus, sovereign God striding across the earth. If God has chosen to celebrate diversity, why don't we? Why do we openly scoff or inwardly roll our eyes when African Americans, womanists, feminists, liberationists, and others come to the table to tell us of their experience of Jesus, to send a message in a bottle to us castaways awaiting news? God gives us opportunities to develop a richer picture of God than that with which we began our journey. Will we shrink away or boldly step forward to accept the gift? No doubt Matthew would have had little tolerance for and would have severely chastised John on a number of counts regarding John's presentation of Jesus. But unlike Matthew's church, we're not a one-Gospel church; we're a four-Gospel church. Praise God.

The multiplicity of voices, both in our Gospels and in our churches, does not result in a cacophony, but rather in a symphony of rich sounds, sometimes exhilarating, sometimes poignant, always gripping. All of the instruments, despite their distinctiveness, play a single piece: Jesus, the Christ. It is this Jesus who walked among us on a small strip of earth two thousand years ago, was crucified, died, and was buried; this Jesus who rose again on the third day and who lives and moves here and now in this place and in every place. It is this Jesus who unifies and this Jesus we confess as Lord. It is this Jesus who is the same yesterday, today, and tomorrow. Come, Lord Jesus.

4

The Synoptic Problem

Some literary relationship exists between Matthew, Mark, and Luke. The puzzle of how they relate constitutes what scholars call "The Synoptic Problem."[1]

EXHIBIT 1: JESUS' BAPTISM

Compare the story of Jesus' Baptism in each of the Synoptics:

Matthew 3:13–17	Mark 1:9–11	Luke 3:21–22
Then Jesus came from Galilee to John at the Jordan, to be baptized by him. John would have prevented him, saying, "I need to be baptized by you, and do you come to me?" But Jesus answered him, "Let it be so now; for it is proper for us in this way to fulfill all righteousness." Then he consented.	In those days Jesus came from Nazareth of Galilee	Now when all the people were baptized,

1. A helpful Web site on the Synoptic Problem is maintained by Stephen Carlson: http://www.mindspring.com/~scarlson/synopt/.

Matthew 3:13–17	Mark 1:9–11	Luke 3:21–22
And when Jesus had been baptized, just as he came up from the water, suddenly the heavens were opened to him and he saw the Spirit of God descending like a dove and alighting on him. And a voice from heaven said, "This is my Son, the Beloved, with whom I am well pleased."	and was baptized by John in the Jordan. And just as he was coming up out of the water, he saw the heavens torn apart and the Spirit descending like a dove on him. And a voice came from heaven, "You are my Son, the Beloved; with you I am well pleased."	and when Jesus also had been baptized and was praying, the heaven was opened, and the Holy Spirit descended upon him in bodily form like a dove. And a voice came from heaven, "You are my Son, the Beloved; with you I am well pleased."

By slowing down and paying attention, the reader discerns both similarities and differences in the accounts. Everything that appears in Mark appears also (a) in *either* Matthew *or* Luke or (b) in *both* Matthew *and* Luke.

Mark and Matthew share the following:

- the mention of Jesus as from Galilee
- the heavens open and the Spirit descends as Jesus comes up out of the water (in Luke this happens *after* Jesus is baptized and is praying)
- John baptizes Jesus and does so at the Jordan

Mark and Luke share the following:

- The voice from heaven speaks directly to Jesus in the second-person singular, "you" (presumably for Jesus' benefit). This is different from Matthew, where the voice speaks about Jesus in the third-person singular, "with whom" (presumably for the benefit of the observers).

Mark shares with *both* Matthew and Luke:

- the fact that Jesus was baptized at some point
- heavens (Luke: heaven) opening
- the Spirit descending like a dove
- a voice from heaven that designates Jesus as "the Beloved Son" in whom "I am well pleased."

Matthew alone has the extra dialogue between John and Jesus, which ends on the theme of Jesus fulfilling all righteousness. Righteousness (Greek: *dikaiosynē*), as it turns out, is one of Matthew's major concerns and emphases throughout the Gospel, much more so than the others.

Luke alone notes that "all the people" were baptized; he also places the descent of the Spirit *after* the baptism, not during that event; finally, he depicts Jesus as in prayer.

Mark is the common denominator between the accounts. It makes sense, then, to suggest that Mark was written first, and that Matthew and Luke, writing later, used Mark as a common source. Consider also that both Matthew and Luke are much longer than Mark and contain much material that is not found in Mark. For instance, Mark begins his Gospel with Jesus as an adult; both Luke and Matthew include stories about Jesus' birth and early years. Luke and Matthew both depict Jesus giving a lengthy sermon (Matt. 5–7: Sermon on the Mount; Luke 6:20–49: Sermon on the Plain). Mark does not contain this sermon. Which is more likely, then, that Matthew and Luke were written first and Mark epitomized them, leaving out such great material as the infancy narratives and the Sermon on the Mount, not to mention the powerful parables of Luke such as the Good Samaritan and the Prodigal Son? Or that Mark was written first, and then Matthew and Luke used Mark and added to Mark from other material to which they had access? Most scholars argue the latter.

EXHIBIT 2: JESUS' REJECTION
IN HIS OWN HOMETOWN

In addition to the fact that Matthew and Luke have considerably more material than Mark, scholars have observed certain theological tendencies that differ in the presentation of, say, Jesus and the disciples. Note the story of Jesus' Rejection in His Own Hometown as told by Mark and Matthew (emphasis added to flag difference):

Matthew 13:58	Mark 6:5–6a
And he *did* not do many deeds of power there, because of their unbelief.	And he *could* do no deed of power there, except that he laid his hands on a few sick people and cured them. And he was amazed at their unbelief.

In Mark's version, Jesus was not able to perform powerful deeds. Matthew, on the other hand, implies that Jesus could have done deeds of power, but chose not to as a reaction to the unbelief of the people. Matthew's Jesus, then, appears to be more powerful. Is it more likely that Matthew changed Mark's version or vice versa? Most would agree that it is more likely that Matthew didn't like Mark's presentation of Jesus as powerless in this instance and, therefore, ascribed more power to Jesus. It seems less likely that Mark, if using Matthew as a source, would have made Jesus less powerful.

EXHIBIT 3: JESUS' STILLING OF THE STORM

The disciples fare better in Matthew and Luke than they do in Mark as the story about Jesus stilling the storm indicates:

Matthew 8:18–27	Mark 4:35–41	Luke 8:22–25
Now when Jesus saw great crowds around him, he gave orders to go over to the other side. [A scribe then approached and said, "Teacher, I will follow you wherever you go." And Jesus said to him, "Foxes have holes, and birds of the air have nests; but the Son of Man has nowhere to lay his head." Another of his disciples said to him, "Lord, first let me go and bury my father." But Jesus said to him, "Follow me, and let the dead bury their own dead."] And when he got into the boat, his disciples followed him. A windstorm arose on the sea, so great that the boat was being swamped by the waves; but he was asleep. And they went and woke him up, saying, "Lord, save us! We are perishing!" And he said to them, "Why are you afraid, you of	On that day, when evening had come, he said to them, "Let us go across to the other side." And leaving the crowd behind, they took him with them in the boat, just as he was. Other boats were with him. A great windstorm arose, and the waves beat into the boat, so that the boat was already being swamped. But he was in the stern, asleep on the cushion; and they woke him up and said to him, "Teacher, do you not care that we are perishing?" He woke up and rebuked the wind, and said to the sea,	One day he got into a boat with his disciples, and he said to them, "Let us go across to the other side of the lake." So they put out, and while they were sailing he fell asleep. A windstorm swept down on the lake, and the boat was filling with water, and they were in danger. They went to him and woke him up, shouting, "Master, Master, we are perishing!" And he woke up and rebuked the wind and the

Matthew 8:18–27	Mark 4:35–41	Luke 8:22–25
little faith?" Then he got up and rebuked the winds and the sea; and there was a dead calm. They were amazed, saying, "What sort of man is this, that even the winds and the sea obey him?"	"Peace! Be still!" Then the wind ceased, and there was a dead calm. He said to them, "Why are you afraid? Have you still no faith?" And they were filled with great awe and said to one another, "Who then is this, that even the wind and the sea obey him?"	raging waves; they ceased, and there was a calm. He said to them, "Where is your faith?" They were afraid and amazed, and said to one another, "Who then is this, that he commands even the winds and the water, and they obey him?"

In Mark, the disciples call Jesus by the mere title "Teacher" and harshly accuse him and question his concern for their well-being: "Don't you care that we're perishing?" Jesus wakes up, rebukes the wind (the same kind of action he uses against demons in the Gospel), and speaks directly to the sea, saying, "Peace! Be still!" Calm ensues. Jesus then notes their fear and accuses the disciples of having no faith. None.

Matthew's version of the story contains some important differences. First, the event does not occur in the same place chronologically in Jesus' ministry. In Mark, Jesus heals the man with the withered hand, indicates who his true relatives are, and tells the parable of the Sower *before* the stilling-of-the-storm event. In Matthew, on the other hand, all of those stories occur *after* the stilling of the storm. So both authors had access to the story but put it in a different place in Jesus' ministry. Luke follows Mark's placement with this event. Embedded within the Matthean version of the story, we also see Jesus' encounter with a scribe and with a disciple, each making a request of Jesus and receiving a response from him. In terms of the content of the story itself, Matthew's disciples wake Jesus up, but they in effect pray to him (rather than castigate him), calling him by the title "Lord" and entreating him to save them. They realize that they need saving, and they know and believe that Jesus has the power to save them. *Salvation*, it turns out, is a heavy theological word for Matthew, as is the title *Lord*. Jesus then notes their fear, but he calls them "you of little faith." This is far softer, of course than "no faith," and it is an expression almost unique to Matthew. It is only after the conversation that Jesus then calms the sea, so even the order of the material within this passage is different from Mark's. We could discuss Luke's version as well, but this is enough for the moment: we see that the same story appears in all three Gospels but is not identical. The evangelists clearly had the freedom to shape their narratives in accordance with their own sensibilities. Matthew repeatedly grants the disciples an elevated status as compared to Mark. In Mark, the disciples are presented as rather obtuse and even opposed to Jesus to some degree.

EXHIBIT 4: JESUS' WALKING ON THE WATER

To drive the point home, let's look at the story of Jesus' Walking on the Water.

Matthew 14:22–34	Mark 6:45–53
Immediately he made the disciples get into the boat and go on ahead to the other side, while he dismissed the crowds. And after he had dismissed the crowds, he went up the mountain by	Immediately he made his disciples get into the boat and go on ahead to the other side, to Bethsaida, while he dismissed the crowd. After saying farewell to them, he went up on the mountain to pray.
himself to pray. When evening came, he was there alone, but by this time the boat, battered by the waves, was far from the land, for the wind was against them. And early in the morning he came walking toward them on the sea. But when the disciples saw him walking on the sea, they were terrified, saying, "It is a ghost!" And they cried out in fear. But immediately Jesus spoke to them and said, "Take heart, it is I; do not be afraid."	When evening came, the boat was out on the sea, and he was alone on the land. When he saw that they were straining at the oars against an adverse wind, he came towards them early in the morning, walking on the sea. He intended to pass them by. But when they saw him walking on the sea, they thought it was a ghost and cried out; for they all saw him and were terrified. But immediately he spoke to them and said, "Take heart, it is I; do not be afraid."
Peter answered him, "Lord, if it is you, command me to come to you on the water." He said, "Come." So Peter got out of the boat, started walking on the water, and came toward Jesus. But when he noticed the strong wind, he became frightened, and beginning to sink, he cried out, "Lord, save me!" Jesus immediately reached out his hand and caught him, saying to him, "You of little faith, why did you doubt?" When they got into the boat, the wind ceased. And those in the boat worshiped him, saying, "Truly you are the Son of God."	Then he got into the boat with them and the wind ceased. And they were utterly astounded, for they did not understand about the loaves, but their hearts were hardened.
When they had crossed over, they came to land at Gennesaret.	When they had crossed over, they came to land at Gennesaret and moored the boat.

Notice that the story does not appear at all in the Gospel of Luke. In both Mark and Matthew, the story begins with Jesus sending the disciples across the water while he prays on a mountain. Early in the morning, Jesus notices the disciples struggling with the wind. Immediately the reader should recall the earlier story of the Stilling of the Storm (Matt. 8:23–27; Mark 4:35–41). Jesus walks out to the disciples. Mark has an odd statement that Jesus "intended to pass them by"; Matthew omits it. In the midst of their fear, Jesus speaks words of assurance to them in both accounts. Then the stories become quite different. In Mark, Jesus enters the boat, the wind ceases, and the disciples are clueless. Actually, they are worse than clueless; their hearts are hardened. At this point Mark is alluding to and comparing the disciples to the Pharaoh of Exodus, who is described by the same terms. Mark has a somewhat cryptic statement: he says they were astounded "for they did not understand about the loaves." Here the author forcefully indicates to the reader that the Gospel is meant to be read as one uninterrupted narrative, just as one would read a novel. This point is often lost on the modern reader who has to deal with the visually disruptive divisions of chapters and verses and subtitles and commentary and notes (all of which are later additions). To get the most out of each Gospel, one must read it from start to finish in order, preferably in a single sitting. Such a reader would immediately recall that just before this incident, Jesus has fed at least 5,000 people—hence the reference to the loaves. Mark indicates that even though the disciples have just witnessed that powerful miracle, they still have no understanding of who Jesus is.

Matthew's version of the story paints the disciples in a much holier light. Instead of the harsh comment about ignorance and hard-heartedness, Matthew tells us that those in the boat "worshiped" Jesus, thus indicating that they do understand who he is: the Son of God (this is a very important title in Matthew's Gospel). Furthermore, Matthew includes a unique story about Peter's walking on water. When he begins to sink, Peter cries out the same prayer we heard earlier in the Stilling of the Storm: "Lord, save me!" And Jesus responds now to Peter alone with the words he earlier used to the whole group: "You of a little faith," why did you doubt? Jesus is able to credit Peter with fledgling faith and teaches him to have more faith. For Matthew, Peter is the primary representative of the disciples; to him Jesus gives the keys to the kingdom (Matt. 16:19). Matthew has more special material devoted to Peter than any other canonical Gospel.

Based on these comparisons, which do you think was written first? Does it make more sense that Mark presented the disciples harshly first and then Matthew elevated them a bit, or that Matthew presented a lofty view of the disciples and then Mark demoted them and eliminated the material about Peter? Most scholars would argue the former.

PROPOSED SOLUTIONS
TO THE SYNOPTIC PROBLEM

Two-Source Hypothesis

The most common solution to the Synoptic Problem among biblical scholars today is known as the Two-Source Hypothesis (it assumes Markan Priority).

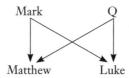

According to this model, Mark was composed first. Matthew and Luke both used Mark. This accounts for the triple tradition: material common to all three Gospels. In addition to Mark, both Matthew and Luke used a source that contained mostly sayings of Jesus. This source is called Q, from the German *Quelle*, meaning "source." This source would have included the sayings that Matthew and Luke share but which do not appear in Mark (some 230 verses), such as the Sermon on the Mount (Plain). Remember the Stilling-of-the-Storm episode? One difference we noticed was Matthew's insertion of two dialogues between Jesus and an interlocutor. These dialogues are missing in Mark altogether but appear in Luke, though not in the middle of the Stilling of the Storm as in Matthew. In fact, hardly any of the sayings shared by Matthew and Luke appear in the same place in the orders of Matthew and Luke.

Matthew 8:18–22	Luke 9:57–60
Now when Jesus saw great crowds around him, he gave orders to go over to the other side. A scribe then approached and said, "Teacher, I will follow you wherever you go." And Jesus said to him, "Foxes have holes, and birds of the air have nests; but the Son of Man has nowhere to lay his head." Another of his disciples said to him, "Lord, first let me go and bury my father." But Jesus said to him, "Follow me, and let the dead bury their own dead."	As they were going along the road, someone said to him, "I will follow you wherever you go." And Jesus said to him, "Foxes have holes, and birds of the air have nests; but the Son of Man has nowhere to lay his head." To another he said, "Follow me." But he said, "Lord, first let me go and bury my father." But Jesus said to him, "Let the dead bury their own dead; but as for you, go and proclaim the kingdom of God."

This is an example of the double tradition: material drawn from a common source (Q) and shared by Luke and Matthew, but not present in Mark. This

Q is a hypothetical document, a scholarly construct, and has not been discovered. The discovery of the *Gospel of Thomas*, roughly contemporaneous with the canonical Gospels, has perhaps given more credence to the existence of such a document as Q since the *Gospel of Thomas* contains nothing but sayings of Jesus. There are 114 sayings in all, some similar to and some distinct from canonical sayings.

But what about the material that is unique to Luke or Matthew? Recall the story about Peter's Walking on Water; it appears nowhere else in the Bible. So also the stories of Herod's Slaughter of the Innocents, the Holy Family's Flight into Egypt, the Earthquake at Jesus' Crucifixion, and so on. For Luke's part, only there does one find the parables of the Prodigal Son, the Good Samaritan, the Rich Fool, the Rich Man and Lazarus, and many others. What sources did Matthew and Luke use for these independent traditions? Scholars refer to each source as M (or "special M") for Matthew, and L (or "special L") for Luke. Adjusting our diagram to include this notion, we see the following lines of influence (and our Two-Source Hypothesis becomes a Four-Source Hypothesis):

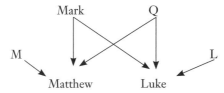

Griesbach Hypothesis (or the Two-Gospel Hypothesis)

Another source-critical hypothesis is known as the Griesbach Hypothesis and suggests that Matthew was written first; Luke wrote second, using Matthew as a source; finally, Mark wrote his Gospel, using the "two Gospels" Matthew and Luke, conflating and epitomizing them. Whereas the Two-Source Hypothesis assumes *Markan* priority, the Two-Gospel Hypothesis assumes *Matthean* priority. Notice that Q does not appear as a source because wherever Matthew and Luke have double tradition material, it's because Luke knows Matthew. In the Two-Source Hypothesis, on the other hand, Matthew and Luke do *not* know each other's writings.

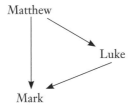

The most notable proponents of this view are Johann Griesbach and William Farmer. This proposal takes into account the few places where Matthew and Luke agree *against* Mark in omissions or alterations of triple-tradition material. Critics of this view wonder, though, why Mark would omit so much of Matthew's and Luke's great material such as the infancy narratives and the Sermon on the Mount (Plain), while simultaneously expanding some stories with insignificant details. Furthermore, if Luke had Matthew, how does one explain the great differences in, say, their infancy narratives and genealogies?

The Farrer Hypothesis

Although the Farrer Hypothesis was out of fashion for some time, yet with some interest in it in England, it has made a vigorous comeback recently thanks to Michael Goulder and Mark Goodacre (the latter of www.ntgateway .com fame). Like the Two-Source Hypothesis but unlike the Griesbach Hypothesis, this assumes *Markan* priority. Like the Griesbach Hypothesis but unlike the Two-Source Hypothesis, it dispenses with Q.

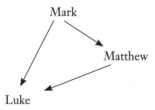

Critics of this hypothesis wonder why Luke would preserve Mark's order while dismissing Matthew's ornate thematic structure.

Form Criticism and Redaction Criticism

So far we've been treating the Gospels in their written form. Jesus died around 30 CE; Paul wrote his letters in the 50s; the Synoptic Gospels are generally dated to 70–90 CE. This means that there's 40 years' worth of material floating around before the first canonical Gospel was penned. Therefore, those who are interested in tracing the historical development of the Bible and the church must inquire after the oral stages of the transmission of the traditions. *Form criticism* is the branch of New Testament studies that attends heavily to that process. Form critics try to discern in what setting (German: *Sitz im Leben*, "setting in life") the individual traditions circulated in the early churches. For instance, the Beatitudes lend themselves to easy memorization, and it's reasonable to assume that the church first used them to catechize new converts. Miracle stories were used to show Jesus' power and authority.

The Lord's Prayer would have been used in worship services. The words of Jesus at the Last Supper would have functioned in a eucharistic setting. In other words, each of the stories and units of material functioned in the church and therefore remained alive and available to the Gospel writers. The Gospel writers (called Evangelists), then, took these various traditions that were circulating orally and combined them to form written narratives. In this view, the Evangelists are considered primarily "stringers of pearls."

But some scholars, called redaction critics, protested what they considered to be a low view of the Evangelists' talents as authors in their own right, who each created a story with a beginning, middle, end, plot, setting, characters, and narrative point of view. Redaction critics argue that each Gospel writer took the independent traditions that the form critics detected and put their own stamp on them by choosing where to place the stories chronologically in Jesus' ministry, how to group them together, which points to emphasize, and how to word them. The evangelist's summaries and authorial choices will often cue the reader to that particular evangelist's major theological concerns and convictions. One of the most effective ways to hear each author is to first read each Gospel in its entirety uninterrupted, noting recurrent language, themes, and style. Then, using a Synopsis or Gospel Parallels, compare passages in the Gospels. As noted, this interpretive methodology is known as *redaction criticism*; it pays attention to the author's own editing of material to discern what the author wants the reader to know or believe about Jesus, church, discipleship, and so on. By employing this method, the interpreter can arrive at such conclusions as "Luke's Jesus shows a special concern for the poor and marginalized of society," or "Matthew's Jesus is very concerned with righteousness." Such a method does *not* claim to know what the historical Jesus actually said or did; rather, it is a literary critical tool that views each Gospel as a finished literary product composed by an early Christian author.

Summary

The shape of Gospel formation, then, looks something like this: Jesus of Nazareth lived from around 4 BCE to around 30 CE. While living, he conducted a ministry of word and deed and gained a following, which we call the Jesus movement. He also made numerous powerful enemies. He was crucified in Jerusalem under Pontius Pilate. His followers believed (and still do) that he was resurrected from the dead and was alive and active in the world. They devoted their lives to following this risen Lord; thus Christianity (rather than the Jesus movement) was born. Stories of Jesus' words and deeds, of his life, death, and resurrection—these Jesus stories circulated for many decades. Paul wrote most of his letters in the 50s CE but mentions surprisingly little about the words and deeds of Jesus. He refers far more to Jesus' death and resurrection. Oddly, he rarely includes any words of Jesus in his various arguments, whether ethical or theological. For instance, when the Corinthian Christians are going at each other, and some of them are using their power to lord it over other members of the church, you might expect Paul to invoke Jesus' words about taking the lowest seat at the table, to cite Jesus on being a servant if one wants to be greatest, or to recount the parable of Lazarus and the Rich Man. But he doesn't. Why not? Does Paul not know these traditions? Did he just decide that wasn't a good technique—to appeal to the words of the Lord?

At some point one or more Christians decided to commit the Jesus traditions to writing in the form of a narrative, thus inventing a new genre called a Gospel. If one follows the Two-Source Hypothesis, one will credit the author of Mark with this feat around 70 CE; if one is a Griesbach devotee, the author of Matthew will receive the honor. It is important to recognize that many other Gospels were composed in the first two centuries and, though they did not wind up in the canon (which was not closed until the end of the 4th century), they were certainly used as authoritative texts by various faithful Christians around the world. (This is not to say that all Christians accepted all of these noncanonical Gospels; some Christian circles tended to use one and others another.) Among the most important are the *Gospel of Thomas*, the *Infancy Gospel of Thomas*, the *Gospel of Mary*, and the *Gospel of Peter*. It's also important to recognize that oral traditions about Jesus did not cease just because some authors committed certain traditions to writing.

The Gospel writers had access to a number of materials, oral and written; each used those sources to shape their own unique presentation of Jesus' life, ministry, and death in accordance with their own (and their community's) theological convictions. These communities were located in different areas of the Mediterranean, with different cultures and congregations. So Matthew's

When elevated church officials issue new decrees, it doesn't mean that their flock suddenly adopts said decree and changes its practices. In 367 CE, Athanasius, bishop of Alexandria, issues his Paschal Letter in which he lists our 27 New Testament books (and only those) and calls them "springs of salvation." The North African Council of Carthage in 397 CE firmly delineated the canon. One can assume that old faithful Christians who recognized the authority of these officials but whose spiritual lives had been shaped by texts such as the Shepherd of Hermas did not all at once consider that text unscriptural. Not to mention certain Christians who did not even recognize the authority of those officials!

community, maybe in Syrian Antioch, would have used Matthew's Gospel; they may not even have been familiar with the existence of Mark, Luke, or John. Likewise, Mark's community, perhaps in Rome, would have used only Mark. John, which we'll turn to in a moment, is often located in Ephesus (modern Turkey). In a way these early churches were fortunate because they did not have to figure out how to handle four different Gospels!

The Synoptics share many similarities. Each narrates at least the baptism of Jesus, some of his teachings, his miracles (including exorcisms, healing, provision of food, controlling the forces of nature), his betrayal, death, and resurrection. But they evince significant differences as well. For instance, Mark has no Annunciation or infancy narrative or stories of Jesus in his early years; Mark starts with Jesus' baptism and temptation in the desert. Where Matthew and Luke tell an extended story of Jesus' temptation in the wilderness by Satan, Mark's version takes only two verses! Many of our favorite parables occur only in Luke. Matthew's Sermon on the Mount and Luke's Sermon on the Plain are not identical: Matthew's Jesus declares, "Blessed are the poor in spirit," whereas Luke's Jesus says, "Blessed are you who are poor." Luke's Jesus says, "Blessed are you who are hungry now, for you will be filled." Luke is focused on present physical need; Matthew moves it to a spiritual plane. Matthew places Jesus' birth in the time of King Herod the Great, who died in 4 BCE. Luke, on the other hand, places the birth in 6 CE, leaving a 10-year discrepancy in Jesus' birth date. Again, this "problem" wouldn't exist if we had only Matthew or Luke.

What are we to make of such differences? Do the evangelists know each other's work? Certainly Luke refers to other accounts of Jesus' life that clearly didn't get the job done well enough; therefore, Luke plans to take a stab at it:

> Since *many* have undertaken to set down an orderly account of the events that have been fulfilled among us, just as they were handed on to us by those who from the beginning were eyewitnesses and servants of the word, *I too decided*, after investigating everything carefully from the very first, *to write an orderly account for you*, most excellent Theophilus, so that you may know with complete security the things about which you have been instructed. (Luke 1:1–4, emphasis added)

Do the Evangelists aim to correct each other? And what happens when we add the Gospel of John to the discussion?

JOHN, THE MAVERICK GOSPEL?

If scholars have a difficult time discerning the relationship among the Synoptics, how much more perplexing the issue becomes when the Gospel of John is added to the mix. John shares enough similarities with the Synoptics to recognize it as a Gospel in the same generic sense: it is a narrative that relates Jesus' life, ministry, death, and resurrection. But John differs significantly from the Synoptics.

Tradition assigns the eagle as the symbol for the author of the Fourth Gospel, whom we'll call John, because only the soaring eagle can stare straight into the sun. And Clement of Alexandria, a 2nd-century church father, said this: "Last of all, John, perceiving that the external facts had been made plain in the [other] Gospels, and being urged by his friends and inspired by the Spirit, composed a spiritual Gospel."

What do moderns have to say about this Gospel, favorite book of Baptists, Catholics, and football-stadium evangelists? Recently I told someone I was writing on the Gospel of John and, as often happens, she said: "Oh, I *love* that Gospel!" I always ask why, so I asked why and she said, "It's so simple." There's one modern opinion! Does your church use a lectionary? Which year is John's year? All years and no year. Is that because it's so simple or because it's too complex?

From the beginning, interpreters of the Fourth Gospel have noticed that it's different, odd, mysterious. Pick up any scholarly work on John, and you'll see phrases such as "puzzle, perplexing, verbal kaleidoscope," and the like. There are problems and puzzles galore that have occupied many great minds, and while scholarship has done much to make John's community real, some folks can't help but feel swept up by the spirit that blows where it wills. If the narratives of the other Gospels can be drawn as a line, John's has to be represented by a dizzying spiral—John uses repetition: over and over one hears a theme introduced, developed later, and revisited with the same words even later. Round and round he drives you until you arrive at the center, and there is simply no doubt that the center for John is Christ and Christ alone. Often John is said to have the "highest" Christology among the Gospels.

For John, Jesus is equal to God. How does John convince you of this? You probably won't be hearing from the Gospel of John this Advent because there's no genealogy, no annunciation, no magi, no birth. John goes straight to the top, taking us back to a time before creation: "In the beginning was the Word, and the Word was with God, and the Word was God. He was in the beginning with God. All things came into being through him, and without him not one thing came into being. What has come into being in him was life, and the life was the light of all people" (John 1:1–4).

In the Synoptics, miracles are called *dynameis*, "deeds of power," a word that never appears in John; in John they are called *sēmeia*, "signs," and of course signs point to something: here they reveal Jesus' true identity and testify to his authority, his origins from God, and the nature of his relationship with God. John narrates seven of Jesus' signs over a three-year ministry.

In contrast to John, a quick skim results in a tally of 20 miracles in Mark over a one-year ministry, in a Gospel that is considerably shorter than the Fourth Gospel.

In this Gospel, Jesus is not baptized by John (and in fact, the author goes to great lengths to subordinate John to Jesus, but that's another story); he suffers no temptation and no agony in the garden; those who come to arrest him fall down in awe; he informs Pilate that Pilate's power is quite puny in comparison to Jesus' power, and so on. Perhaps most perplexing, Jesus dies on a different day in the Gospel of John. By the time he is eating the Last Supper with the disciples in the Synoptics, he's already dead in John.

What is John's relationship to the Synoptics? Does the author aim to supplement, complement, correct, or replace the Synoptics? Does the author even know the Synoptic Gospels? None of the Gospel authors identify themselves in the texts, so we cannot know for certain who penned them. The original texts do not have titles; in fact they don't even have chapter and verse demarcations and certainly no subheadings such as "The parable of the Good Samaritan," as many of us find in our Bibles today. All of those are later additions. Thus it is impossible to know exactly who the authors were and what they did and did not know about the other Gospels circulating.

IMPORTANT ISSUES RAISED

Stephen Carlson has called the Synoptic Problem "the cornerstone of historical-critical scholarship of the gospels." He argues that "one's solution to the synoptic problem will influence one's exegesis, redaction criticism, and form criticism of the gospels as well as affect the quest for the historical Jesus, early church history, and even the text of the gospels."[2] In what follows I'll suggest some of the issues raised by pondering the Synoptic Problem.

1. I Love to TELL (Not *Write*) the Story, For Some Have Never Heard (Not *Read*)

James D. G. Dunn complains about the literary default mode by which modern New Testament scholars operate, a setting that he says "has contorted the way we envisage the early transmission of the Jesus tradition."[3] Theories about the Synoptic Problem present a *linear* model of development, which is not defensible. We enjoy high literacy rates; the 1st-century Mediterranean

2. Ibid.
3. James D. G. Dunn, *A New Perspective on Jesus: What the Quest for the Historical Jesus Missed* (Grand Rapids: Baker Academic, 2005), 125.

world had low literacy rates. People heard stories, memorized them, and passed them on orally. The Synoptic Problem focuses far too heavily upon literary sources in its reconstruction of the way the Christian tradition developed. Dunn himself finds the Two-Source Hypothesis reasonable. Where that hypothesis fails to account for particular agreements or disagreements within the Synoptics, he asks us to consider oral-source explanations rather than simply devising literary theories about multiple written versions of each Gospel, layers of composition, and so forth. In an oral culture, the traditions about Jesus would have been characterized from the beginning as both fixed and flexible. Traditions that mattered would have been told and retold, and this would surely have entailed some variation, depending upon the teller/performer. On the other hand, the fact that these particular traditions would have been told so often would have given them some fixed shape. Think of the Lord's Prayer (which, by the way, we say differently today from the way it is recorded in Matthew and Luke—see for yourself at Matt. 6:9–13 and Luke 11:1–4) or the Words of Institution (Mark 14:22–25; Luke 22:17–20; Matt. 26:26–29; 1 Cor. 11:23–26)—surely Matthew and Luke knew of these traditions from participating in their church communities, not simply from looking at Mark's written text. Dunn's appeal to orality to explain some of the differences we discover in the Synoptics, including even Jesus' words and deeds, does not mean he finds no stability in the tradition:

> In oral tradition there is characteristically a tale to be told, a teaching to be treasured, in and through and precisely by means of the varied performances. Oral tradition is oral memory; its primary function is to preserve and recall what is of importance from the past. Tradition, more or less by definition, embodies the concern for continuity with the past, a past drawn upon but also enlivened that it might illuminate the present and future. In the words of E. A. Havelock, "Variability and stability, conservatism and creativity, evanescence and unpredictability all mark the pattern of oral transmission." . . . It is this combination that makes it possible for the community both to acknowledge its tradition and to delight in the freshness of the individual performance.[4]

What's the payoff of Dunn's argument?

> Perhaps the point most to be emphasized in conclusion is that to recognize the character of the Jesus tradition as oral tradition is to recognize its character also as *living tradition*. The Jesus tradition was not at first a written text, to be read by individuals in the solitude of their studies, capable of fine literary analysis and redaction. It was not

4. Ibid., 98–99.

carried around like a sacred relic fixed in written form. It was living tradition, lived-in-and-through tradition. It was not so much kept as used, not so much preserved as performed, not so much read as heard. To treat it as a lifeless artifact, suitable for clinical dissection, is to lose it. Its variability, the oral principle of "variation within the same," is not a sign of degeneration or corruption. Rather, it puts us directly in touch with the tradition in its living character, as it was heard in the earliest Christian groups and churches, and can still be heard and responded to today.[5]

Let's assume the Two-Source Hypothesis (with Q and Markan priority), since it seems to account for more of the evidence than do the other hypotheses (though *none* of the hypotheses can account for all of the data without remainder). Note that even after Mark put the story into writing, oral traditions about Jesus continued to circulate; Matthew and Luke surely drew upon oral traditions. And the fact of so many other gospels (*Gospel of Mary*, *Gospel of Peter*, *Gospel of Thomas*, etc.; cf. Luke's reference to many other Gospels in Luke 1:1) that did not, finally, make it into the canon shows that oral traditions continued to circulate well into the 2nd century.

2. Q Questions and Critiques

Proponents of Q (think ancient texts, not Jean-Luc Picard and his nemesis of Star Trek fame) have had a field day in recent years, resulting in a critical edition of Q modeled in some ways on the Nestle-Aland critical edition of the Greek New Testament. The International Q Project (IQP) has produced important scholarship, especially under the leadership of James M. Robinson and John S. Kloppenborg.[6] Q scholars have moved into deep levels of detail about the "Q Community," its chronological development over time, its ethics, its Christology, and so on.

But not everyone is convinced about Q and Q scholarship.

a. Everyone, including Q proponents, must remember that Q is a hypothetical document. A copy of Q has never been discovered. This can be confusing since you can hold the *Critical Edition* in your hands now. That is a scholarly construct based on verses shared in common between Luke and Matthew.

b. We are now up to the 27th edition of Nestle-Aland's *Novum Testamentum Graece*; presumably Q scholars will continue to research and debate and

---

5. Ibid., 125.

6. James M. Robinson, ed., *The Sayings Gospel Q: Collected Essays*, Bibliotheca ephermeridum theologicarum lovaniensium 189 (Leuven: Leuven University Press, 2005). James M. Robinson, Paul Hoffman, and John S. Kloppenborg, *The Critical Edition of Q: Synopsis Including the Gospels of Matthew and Luke, Mark and Thomas with English, German, and French Translations of Q and Thomas*, Hermeneia (Minneapolis: Fortress Press, 2000).

refine their criteria as they produce future editions.[7] Indeed, in a recent paper Jeffrey Peterson argued that by their own criteria, the Q scholars should identify material from Jesus' birth, passion, and resurrection. This would amount to adding Q 1:30–31; 22:63–64; and 24:33–49, following the tradition of naming Q passages according to Luke's versification.

c. William Farmer devoted his entire academic career to the Synoptic Problem. As indicated by the title of one of his books, *The Gospel of Jesus: The Pastoral Relevance of the Synoptic Problem*,[8] Farmer finds the very truth of the Gospel at stake in this debate. He argues that the Two-Source Hypothesis grants Q more authority as a historical source than the canonical Gospels themselves. And given that Q has always been envisioned as a "sayings source," Jesus' death and resurrection are belittled as inconsequential elements of the tradition from its inception. Let me give you a feel for his passion about the issue:

> The final chapter of this book attempts to address the question of what difference it makes whether one adheres to the commonly accepted Two-Source Hypothesis or the less popular, but perhaps more credible, Two-Gospel Hypothesis. The church at its best will always strive to "get it straight." We must never forget what happened to the "quest for truth" in the universities of the Third Reich. A "critically correct" civil religion, pushed by university-trained German-Christian theologians like Emmanuel Hirsch, gloried in the idea of Markan priority with its understanding of Christian theology based on the Two-Source Hypothesis, while Christians who witnessed unto blood and resisted unto death the Nazi horrors that led to the Holocaust drew spiritual support from a reading of the Gospels that called them to be saints and martyrs of the church (an understanding of Christ called for by any hypothesis that recognizes the primary character of the Matthean text). This is the difference. This is what is at stake for the church.[9]

And on a less bombastic, less dramatic note:

> The Two-Gospel Hypothesis not only makes more sense of the "facts on the ground," but also more adequately accounts for the church's tradition concerning the Gospel narratives and, not insignificantly, allows Christians greater confidence as believing readers that the

7. Jeffrey Peterson, "Jesus' Annunciation, Abuse, and Appearance to the Eleven: Three Neglected Pericopes of the 'Sayings Gospel Q' (Q 1:30–31; 22:63–64; and 24:33–49)," presented to the Seminar on the Development of Early Catholic Christianity at Southern Methodist University on February 4, 2010. Peterson himself actually is a proponent of the Farrer Hypothesis, not of Q.

8. William Farmer, *The Gospel of Jesus: The Pastoral Relevance of the Synoptic Problem* (Louisville, KY: Westminster/John Knox Press, 1994).

9. Ibid., 8.

character and message of Jesus Christ has been faithfully transmitted to them.[10]

Farmer certainly helps us to consider some of the possible shortcomings of the Two-Source Hypothesis. But it's important to note that, in my opinion, he is railing not so much against scholars who use the Two-Source Hypothesis (which most mainstream scholars do), but those who combine the Two-Source Hypothesis with deep dependency on the *Gospel of Thomas* and argue that both Q and the *Gospel of Thomas* predate the canonical Gospels. This allows them to reconstruct the earliest layer of Christianity from sources that are not canonical and end up with a Jesus whose death and resurrection do not matter for the earliest Christians but were added as important by "later" (read "inferior") sources, such as Matthew and Luke. So, reader, be careful to distinguish between those scholars who rely loosely on the Two-Source Hypothesis and remain cautious about how far to press Q, and those who are enamored of Q and posit a whole community with stages, and so forth. No matter which hypothesis a scholar chooses, however, it would be inaccurate and unhelpful to compare them and their investigations to the Third Reich. Christians of equal intellect, discipline, and commitment to the Christian faith genuinely disagree, Hitler notwithstanding.

d. Mark Goodacre argues for Markan priority without Q. Early in his book, *The Case against Q*, he writes:

> If we were to dispense with Q, it would not be without tears. For Q has been all over the world, loved by everyone, feminists and liberation theologians, the sober and the sensational, the scholar and the layperson, a document with universal appeal. Indeed one of the keys to its success has been its ability to woo both conservatives and radicals alike. While conservatives, for example, are drawn by its early witness to sayings of Jesus, others have seen its lack of a Passion Narrative as witnessing to an alternative stream of early Christianity, one not based on the proclamation of a crucified Christ. For those at one end of the theological spectrum, Q can give us a document of Jesus material from before 70, written within a generation of the death of Jesus. For those at the other end of the spectrum, Q aligns itself with the Gospel of Thomas to form a "trajectory" in early Christianity that contrasted radically with emerging orthodoxy, and which only "canonical bias" can now obscure from our view.[11]

Goodacre proceeds to problematize and argue against Q. Not to ruin the ending for you, but in his epilogue he notes five implications of dispensing with Q:

10. Ibid., 188–89.
11. Mark Goodacre, *The Case against Q: Studies in Markan Priority and the Synoptic Problem* (Harrisburg, PA: Trinity Press International, 2002), 16–17.

1. Gospel of Thomas: it affects the study of the Gospel of Thomas, which has too long been tethered to Q.

2. Genre considerations: Markan priority with Luke's knowledge of Matthew changes the way we view the growth and development of the Gospel genre; it also invites fresh consideration of how the canonical Gospels interact with each other.

3. Oral traditions: much like Dunn, Goodacre would have us attend more closely to the role of oral traditions in the development of the Synoptics.

4. Matthean studies: without Q, where did Matthew get his/her non-Markan material?

5. Lukan studies: if Luke used Mark and Matthew, why did he or she change the material so extensively? What literary rationale drove Luke?

"But the Q hypothesis has served us well, and it is with a lump in our throats that we bid it adieu. Q stands as a monument that reminds us of many of the advances made in biblical scholarship over the last 150 years."[12]

3. Dear John

The Gospel of John has been in the Christian canon as long as the Synoptic Gospels have. How is it, then, that for over a century scholars who have a love affair with "getting it straight" (Farmer's words) regarding the development of the Christian faith and the literary genre of Gospels, and the interaction among the canonical Gospels (not to mention the Historical Jesus)—these scholars have not only failed to notice the Gospel of John; they have also intentionally broken up with it?

You, the reader, should question the assumption that John does not naturally fit into the Synoptic Problem and all of its attendant issues. D. Moody Smith has spent a vast amount of his career on the relationship among John and the Synoptics, insisting upon the independence of John's tradition.[13] In his recent work, *The Fourth Gospel and the Quest for Jesus: Modern Foundations Reconsidered*, Paul Anderson has advanced our thinking and sparked our imaginations about the distinctive ways John relates to each of the Gospel traditions.[14] This is particularly true of "Part III: Interfluential, Formative and Dialectical—A Theory of John's Relation to the Synoptics." He argues for an "interfluential set of relationships" during the oral stages of Mark's and John's

12. Ibid., 189.
13. D. Moody Smith, *John among the Gospels*, Second Edition (Columbia: University of South Carolina Press, 2001).
14. Paul Anderson, *The Fourth Gospel and the Quest for Jesus: Modern Foundations Reconsidered* (London: T&T Clark, 2006).

Dear John,

   Thank you so much for all the ways you have enriched us over the centuries. We have taken your words to heart and been moved; our minds have been provoked to deeper thought. We have encountered Jesus in your text; we have watched faithful apostles like the Samaritan woman and Mary Magdalene spread the word about you. We have been called to deep faith, and we've learned a lot about the history of the 1st century. But now we must send you on your way for we have decided, based on unfounded yet unequivocal "conventional wisdom," that you are not as true as our other love: the Synoptic Gospels. They alone can teach us about the earliest (and therefore "truest") instantiations of the Christian faith. They alone show us the *real* Jesus(es). No matter that you seem to have so much in common with the material in the Synoptics; no matter that, if we truly analyzed our assumptions, we would see that you have just as much claim to harboring the earliest layers of the tradition (or we could at least go through the rigorous academic process of why that *cannot* be the case). You are just John, a "spiritual Gospel." You should meet our other love, the Synoptics. Surely you've never met them, but we think you'd agree with them in some ways. Well, attending to you is taking us away from our soulmate, so we must bid you a fond farewell.

   Warmly,

   The Biblical Guild

traditions. John augments and perhaps even corrects Mark. Anderson then argues that John exerts a "formative influence" on Luke and Lukan theology, and even upon Q, if there was a Q. He sees John's relationship to Matthew as "reinforcing, dialectical and corrective." In his "Bi-Optic Hypothesis," Anderson argues that while Matthew and Luke built upon Mark, John built around Mark.

   In short, it's a new day in the study of the Synoptic Problem, and the issues are indeed extremely important ones for Christians and the way they construe their faith.

STUDY QUESTIONS

1. Have you ever spent time with one biblical story in the Synoptics and noticed the differences and similarities between them before reading this chapter? What about the experience challenged your understanding of Scripture? What challenged your faith? What strengthened your faith?

2. What do you think of the scholarly production of a Q Gospel? What questions would you have for the scholars who created this work?
3. Do you think John had access to one or more of the Synoptic Gospels? Why, or why not?
4. What are the implications for your church community in considering the different priority hypotheses of the Gospels? Does it change how you view the authority of Mark (considering the Two-Source Hypothesis) or the authority of Matthew (considering the Griesbach Hypothesis)? How does this question impact the authority of the Gospel of John?

5

Authorship Issues

The Pauline Trajectory

Did Paul write Ephesians? The Pastorals? If not, in what way are those texts scriptural? Most scholars identify only seven epistles as indubitably Pauline: Romans, 1 and 2 Corinthians, Galatians, Philippians, Philemon, and 1 Thessalonians. Many consider 2 Thessalonians to be authentic. Few ascribe Colossians, Ephesians, and the Pastorals to Paul, and still fewer count Paul as the writer of Hebrews. Yet I routinely hear pastors, laity, and seminarians ascribe all of the above to "the blessed apostle."

Why are many scholars reluctant to assign the so-called deuteropauline letters to Paul? Why is the church so reluctant to accept the conclusions of scholars on this matter? Your view of the authorship issue affects your reconstruction of the historical and doctrinal development of the church as well as your estimation of Paul as a theologian and pastor. For instance, how do you adjudicate between the charismatic leadership, imminent eschatology, and advice about marriage in the Corinthian material on the one hand and, on the other hand, the church offices, the more realized eschatology, and the encouragement of marriage and childbearing in Ephesians and the Pastorals? Does Paul contradict himself, or does his thought merely "develop"? Or is it more likely that disciples committed to Paul penned the disputed epistles? If so, do these constitute spurious documents? Or are they faithful witnesses to what the apostle would have said if he had lived to experience the delay of the Parousia? If they are not written by Paul, how much weight should they be given in Christian formation and praxis? The issue relates to all of the New Testament texts. Did "Matthew" write Matthew? Did the apostle Peter write 1 and 2 Peter? Did the author of the Fourth Gospel write Revelation? Should we care? Why or why not?

WHAT DID PAUL WRITE?

Thirteen books of the New Testament claim Paul and his coworkers as
authors:

- Romans (alone)
- 1 Corinthians (with Sosthenes)
- 2 Corinthians (with Timothy)
- Galatians (with "all the members of God's family who are with me")
- Ephesians (alone)
- Philippians (with Timothy)
- Colossians (with Timothy)
- 1 Thessalonians (with Silvanus and Timothy)
- 2 Thessalonians (with Silvanus and Timothy)
- the so-called Pastoral Epistles: 1 and 2 Timothy and Titus (all three
  alone)
- Philemon (with Timothy)

No scholar would contest the authorship of Romans, 1 and 2 Corinthians, Galatians, Philippians, Philemon, and 1 Thessalonians. The remaining
books are questionable. Why? Largely due to language, style, and theology.
Take, for example, the topics of eschatology, the relationship between Jews
and Christians, gender issues, and church offices.

Eschatology

Eschatology has to do with "last things" (from Greek *eschatos*, "last" + *logos*,
"word"). In Paul's day, many forms of Judaism maintained an apocalyptic
eschatology. Paul himself held such a view, which is often characterized by
the following features:[1]

- urgent expectation of the end of earthly conditions in the immediate
  future
- the end as a cosmic catastrophe
- periodization and determinism
- activity of angels and demons
- new salvations, paradisal in character
- manifestation of the kingdom of God
- a mediator with royal functions: a messiah (Hebrew: "anointed"; used of
  OT kings)
- the catchword "glory"

---

1. See John J. Collins, *The Apocalyptic Imagination: An Introduction to Jewish Apocalyptic Literature* (Grand Rapids: Wm. B. Eerdmans Pub. Co., 1998), 12.

- the conviction that the end time will match the primeval time (as in the German phrase scholars often use: *Endzeit gleicht Urzeit*); so Revelation speaks of a "new heaven and a new earth" (21:1). It's language of restoration and redemption (not obliteration of the earth) that the authors have in mind.[2]
- There will be judgment, including punishment for the wicked and reward for the righteous; these groups are considered to be distinct, with no overlap (see Matt. 25:32–46). God will come swiftly and decisively to deal with human sin; Paul refers to this as "the coming wrath" in 1 Thessalonians (1:10).
- The worldview is dualistic and is usually held by socially distressed groups. It's not surprising then that adherents anticipate the *great reversal* (the rich become poor and the poor become rich, those who suffer will rejoice and those who rejoice will suffer, those in power become powerless and the lowly are exalted).

In the undisputed Pauline Epistles, Paul expects the Parousia, the (second) coming of Jesus, imminently. He tells Christians in Corinth that "the present form [*schēma*] of this world is passing away" (1 Cor. 7:31). The time has grown short, and he wants everyone's attention upon Jesus. He wishes that no one would marry, and he certainly does not want Christians to procreate since it would interfere with utter devotional focus. He concedes that it's not an actual sin to marry, but it is far from his wishes. Marriage, it turns out, is only for those who cannot keep their hands off one another, those whom lust has overtaken: "To the unmarried and the widows I say that it is well for them to remain unmarried as I am. But if they are not practicing self-control, they should marry. For it is better to marry than to be aflame with passion" (1 Cor. 7:8–9). Hardly a sacramental view of marriage!

And consider 1 Corinthians 7:20–32:

> Let each of you remain in the condition in which you were called.
> Were you a slave when called? Do not be concerned about it. Even if you can gain your freedom, make use of your present condition now more than ever. For whoever was called in the Lord as a slave is a freed person belonging to the Lord, just as whoever was free when called is a slave of Christ. You were bought with a price; do not become slaves of human masters. In whatever condition you were called, brothers and sisters, there remain with God.
> Now concerning virgins, I have no command of the Lord, but I give my opinion as one who by the Lord's mercy is trustworthy. *I think that, in view of the impending crisis, it is well for you to remain as you are.* Are you bound to a wife? Do not seek to be free. Are you free from a wife? Do not seek a wife. But if you marry, you do not sin, and

2. Barbara Rossing, *The Rapture Exposed: The Message of Hope in the Book of Revelation* (Boulder, CO: Westview Press, 2005).

> if a virgin marries, she does not sin. Yet those who marry will experi-
> ence distress in this life, and I would spare you that. *I mean, brothers*
> *and sisters, the appointed time has grown short; from now on, let even those*
> *who have wives be as though they had none,* and those who mourn as
> though they were not mourning, and those who rejoice as though
> they were not rejoicing, and those who buy as though they had no
> possessions, and those who deal with the world as though they had
> no dealings with it. *For the present form of this world is passing away.*
> (emphasis added)

So sure is the apostle that Jesus will return imminently that he asks his
people to remain as they are: married, unmarried, or slave. Clearly Paul did
not imagine there was time to rehabilitate entire social systems before the end
would come. Would he have spoken differently if he had known we'd still be
here 2,000 years later?

This eschatology characterizes each of the undisputed letters. Read 1 Thessalonians. Paul has taught the Thessalonians that Jesus will return promptly.
Therefore, confusion arises for them when some of their church members
die. Does this mean that those who have died will not be included in the kingdom? Paul tries to quell their fears:

> But we do not want you to be uninformed, brothers and sisters, about
> those who have died, so that you may not grieve as *others* do *who have*
> *no hope*. For since we believe that Jesus died and rose again, even so,
> through Jesus, God will bring with him those who have died. For this
> we declare to you by the word of the Lord, that we who are alive,
> who are left until the coming of the Lord, will by no means precede
> those who have died. For the Lord himself, with a cry of command,
> with the archangel's call and with the sound of God's trumpet, will
> descend from heaven, and the dead in Christ will rise first. Then we
> who are alive, who are left, will be caught up in the clouds together
> with them to meet the Lord in the air; and so we will be with the
> Lord forever. Therefore encourage one another with these words.
> (1 Thess. 4:13–18)

Paul goes on to remind them that this second coming will come like a thief in
the night, so the Christians should be watchful and expectant (5:1–11).

Second Thessalonians, on the other hand, seems to undermine the urgency
of the Parousia (2:2). It would appear that these Christians took Paul's teaching about the imminence of Christ's coming so seriously that they stopped
their regular lives to wait for the Lord. Think of those groups in modern
times who expect the end to come and sell everything and gather on a hilltop
for the magical moment. This author is impatient with such an approach. He
wants them to get back to work and carry on with their lives (2 Thess. 3:6–12),
knowing that at some point Christ will come, but not yet. It is difficult to

decide whether or not 2 Thessalonians is pseudonymous. Oddly, its close similarity to 1 Thessalonians raises suspicions about its authenticity. Either Paul wrote it so soon after 1 Thessalonians that he remembers his language verbatim, or a pseudonymous author slavishly copies Paul's style (one-third of 1 Thessalonians appears in 2 Thessalonians). As in some of the other disputed letters, the eschatology raises real questions. What does the future look like for Christians? What is the goal toward which (salvation) history is moving? Will there be an end to life on earth as we know it? If so, when? Will there be warning signs?

Colossians and Ephesians share a literary relationship and can therefore be treated together. Both are marked by what is called a *realized eschatology*: there is more focus on the present reality and benefits of salvation rather than the future unfolding of it. What Paul takes on faith in Christ's future final acts, the author of Ephesians considers to be already completed. In Romans 6:5–8 and 1 Corinthians 15:21–23, Paul speaks of the *future* time when we will be raised with Christ; in Ephesians, the author considers that a present reality already and thus uses the past tense in 2:4–7: "But God, who is rich in mercy, out of the great love with which he loved us even when we were dead through our trespasses, *made* us alive together with Christ—by grace you have been saved—and *raised us up* with him and *seated us* with him in the heavenly places in Christ Jesus" (emphasis added). And the author of Colossians, sounding much like Ephesians, writes: "When you *were buried* with him in baptism, you *were also raised* with him through faith in the power of God, who raised him from the dead" (2:12, emphasis added). Whereas Paul in 1 Corinthians 15:23–28 envisions the future day when God *will* put all things under Christ's feet, for the author of Ephesians, this has already occurred, as in 1:22–23: "And he has put all things under his feet and has made him the head over all things for the church. . . ."

Jewish-Christian Relations in Paul

One example of something future for Paul but already completed for the author of Ephesians is the tension between Judaism and Christianity (in Paul's time a form of Judaism, but by the time of Ephesians something more distinct from Judaism). As a Pharisaic Jewish Christian, Paul constantly anguishes over the relationship between Judaism and Christianity. By divine election Israel was chosen. It's not as though God decided to hold a contest among the nations to see who would win the right to be God's chosen people and Israel won. Election is God's prerogative, and God initiated the process by God's own volition and accord. That's all well and good. But what happens when (a) God's chosen Messiah ends up crucified by Rome and (b) not all Jews believe in that Messiah? Does God revoke God's covenant with Israel? If so, does that mean that God is not faithful to God's promises? Can human beings occlude the will of God? Romans, especially chapters 9–11, evinces Paul's most impassioned treatment of these questions. There Paul fervently appeals to logic and metaphor and autobiography and poetry to make sense of it all. In the end, he accedes to mystery: "O the depth of the riches and wisdom and knowledge of God! How unsearchable are his judgments and how inscrutable his ways!

> 'For who has known the mind of the Lord?
>   Or who has been his counselor?'
> 'Or who has given a gift to him,
>   to receive a gift in return?'

For from him and through him and to him are all things. To him be the glory forever. Amen" (11:33–12:1).

To feel the urgency of the question for Paul, read these other passages from Romans:

> I am speaking the truth in Christ—I am not lying; my conscience confirms it by the Holy Spirit—I have great sorrow and unceasing anguish in my heart. For I could wish that I myself were accursed and cut off from Christ for the sake of my own people, my kindred according to the flesh. They are Israelites, and to them belong the adoption, the glory, the covenants, the giving of the law, the worship, and the promises; to them belong the patriarchs, and from them, according to the flesh, comes the Messiah, who is over all, God blessed forever. Amen.
> It is not as though the word of God had failed. (Rom. 9:1–6)
> I ask, then, has God rejected his people? By no means! I myself am an Israelite, a descendant of Abraham, a member of the tribe of Benjamin. God has not rejected his people whom he foreknew. Do you not know what the scripture says of Elijah, how he pleads with God against Israel? "Lord, they have killed your prophets, they have demolished your altars; I alone am left, and they are seeking my life." But what is the divine reply to him? "I have kept for myself seven thousand who have not bowed the knee to Baal." So too at the present time there is a remnant, chosen by grace. But if it is by grace, it is no longer on the basis of works, otherwise grace would no longer be grace.
> What then? Israel failed to obtain what it was seeking. The elect obtained it, but the rest were hardened, as it is written,

> > "God gave them a sluggish spirit,
> >   eyes that would not see
> >   and ears that would not hear,
> > down to this very day."

And David says,

> "Let their table become a snare and a trap,
>   a stumbling block and a retribution for them;
> let their eyes be darkened so that they cannot see,
>   and keep their backs forever bent."

> So I ask, have they stumbled so as to fall? By no means! But through
> their stumbling salvation has come to the Gentiles, so as to make
> Israel jealous. Now if their stumbling means riches for the world, and
> if their defeat means riches for Gentiles, how much more *will* their
> full inclusion mean! (Rom. 11:1–13)

The reconciliation of Jew and Christian and God's covenant lies in the
(near) future for Paul. It's a live issue for him. By the time you get to Ephesians 2:11–18, the issue seems to have been resolved.

Gender Issues

Those who doubt the Pauline authorship of Colossians, Ephesians, and the
Pastoral Epistles (1 and 2 Timothy and Titus) also point to the disparity in
attitudes toward women exhibited by the texts. Much has been written about
this subject, and I encourage you to explore it in detail. Let me simply provide
some broad strokes. While it's true that Paul's imminent eschatology left him
largely unconcerned with overhauling society outside the church, you can
discern from the undisputed epistles a profound egalitarian visionary insight
on Paul's part stated most powerfully in Galatians:

> As many of you as were baptized into Christ have clothed yourselves
> with Christ. There is no longer Jew or Greek, there is no longer slave
> or free, there is no longer male and female; for all of you are one in
> Christ Jesus. (3:27–28)

Here Paul makes it clear that, in God's eyes, distinctions that humans
make on the basis of race and religion (such as Jew/Greek), social class (slave
or free), and gender constructs (male and female) are simply that: human
constructs that divide and provide hierarchies where God intends unity and
equality. This radical vision appears to have been borne out in his own ministry. At every turn one finds women acting as apostles (Junia, in Rom. 16:7),
ministers (Phoebe, in Rom. 16:1–2), prophets (1 Cor. 11), leaders of house
churches (the only kind of churches that existed in Paul's day; check out
Chloe in 1 Cor. 1:11), and prominent teachers (Priscilla, in Rom. 16:3–4;
1 Cor. 16:19). In short, women served the same functions as men since Paul's
view of leadership was charismatically based.

What do I mean by "charismatically based"? Perhaps it is best described by Paul himself in 1 Corinthians 12. Here Paul explains that each and every Christian has been gifted by God in some way *for the edification of the church*. Some are called to be teachers, some have the gift of hospitality, some are musicians, and some have a special gift for working with children. *Charisma* is the Greek word for "spiritual gift," and Paul trusts that in any Christian body God has provided the necessary gifts for that community to function for the spread of the gospel, to the glory of God. Gifts are not provided on the basis of gender, race, ethnicity, class, age, and so forth. People, not God, add those limitations and heavy yoke to God's plan.

Colossians, Ephesians, and the Pastorals have quite a different view of gender, however. In Colossians and Ephesians (and 1 Peter, for that matter), one finds "household codes" (German: *Haustafeln*), a common form of Greek philosophical literature that prescribes how each member of a household hierarchy should behave. Caesar occupies the very top rung. The husband/father/master is under Caesar but over everyone in his own household, for as Arius Didymus wrote: "A man has the rule of this household by nature, for the deliberative faculty in a woman is inferior, in children it does not yet exist, and in the case of slaves, it is completely absent." Next comes the mother/wife, the children, and the slaves, in that order. Slaves were broken into two groups: those enslaved by being captured in war and those who are slaves "by nature" who are "strong in body for service, but stupid and unable to live by [themselves], for whom slavery is beneficial."[3] When the eldest male child reached the age of majority, he rose above the mother in the hierarchy. The oft-quoted Ephesians 5:22–6:9 (as well as Colossians 3:18, 22) enjoins wives to submit to their husbands and slaves to obey their masters. The husband is said to be the head of the wife. Not surprisingly, the paterfamilias typically determined the religion of the household. For women and slaves to opt for a different religion was to undermine the authority of the head of the household.

This "Paul" of Ephesians and Colossians is difficult to harmonize with the apostle who preached Galatians 3:27–28 and who considered Junia, Phoebe, Chloe, and a host of other women to be powerful purveyors of the gospel independent of husbands. Recall 1 Corinthians 7, where Paul implores women *not* to get married so that they may devote themselves to serving Christ wholeheartedly. So famous was Paul for this conviction that the *Acts of Paul and Thecla* was produced and beloved and held as scriptural by many early Christians. Thecla, after hearing Paul's preaching, took him at his word and decided not

---

3. Arius Didymus, *Epitome of Stoic Ethics*, in Stobaeus, *Florilegium*.

to marry but rather to spend her days preaching the gospel. This angered her betrothed, Thamyris, as well as her mother (who implored the authorities to burn her daughter to death to set an example for other young women not to opt out of their defined social roles) and led to the persecution of both Paul and Thecla for upsetting the "natural" social order. If you've never read it, stop now and do so![4] You won't be sorry; it's an entertaining, short read.

What appears to have happened in the early church is something like this: Jesus, and Paul after him, brought a message about the reign of God that was countercultural and brought into question, among other things, the justice of contemporary social structures vis-à-vis God's own vision. Both followed a model of charismatic leadership, and both expected the imminent eschaton, the end, when God would set all things right and make good on God's promises of redemption, upon which the hope of all Christians rests.

As it happened, the Parousia did not occur early on. This raised the dilemma referred to as the delay of the Parousia. In a nutshell, the early church realized that the world did not seem to be ending soon, so they had to start thinking about how to endure as a church in the world for the long haul. As the church became an increasingly centralized institution structured and dependent upon particular offices rather than charismatic leadership, it accommodated and adapted the social structures of its host culture, the Roman Empire. This led to the suppression of women in church leadership and a call for women to get married, get pregnant, and tend to their families—in short, to move from the public to the private sphere. Modern churches have inherited this legacy and apparently continue to struggle with the correctness of women as leaders in churches.

This combination of the institutionalization of the church and the drive to keep women "in their place" is particularly evident in the Pastoral Epistles. According to the author of the Pastorals, women are particularly obtuse and susceptible to being led astray: "For among them are those who make their way into households and captivate *silly* women, overwhelmed by their sins and swayed by all kinds of desires, who are *always* being instructed and can *never* arrive at a knowledge of the truth" (2 Tim. 3:6–8, emphasis added). Strong language indeed. Instead of Paul's call for women (and men as well) to avoid marriage if at all possible, the author of the Pastorals commands quite the opposite. And where Paul expects women to pray and prophesy in church (1 Cor. 11), the author of 1 Timothy implores women to shut up in church:

> Let a woman learn in silence with full submission. I permit no woman
> to teach or to have authority over a man; she is to shut up. For Adam

4. See http://wesley.nnu.edu/biblical_studies/noncanon.

was formed first, then Eve; and Adam was not deceived, but the
woman was deceived and became a transgressor. Yet *she will be saved
through childbearing*, provided they continue in faith and love and
holiness, with modesty. (2:11–15, emphasis added)

Gone is Paul's conviction that everyone is saved by grace through faith;
for this author, women are saved through childbearing. If Paul doesn't want
women to marry, how much less so would he want them to bear children?
And presumably, one cannot simultaneously prophesy and shut up in church.

Church Offices

One does not need church offices if Jesus is coming back tomorrow, but if the
church is to endure in the world over centuries, it may require structure. In
response to such a perceived need, a genre of literature emerged in the 2nd
century CE known as *church orders*.[5] These texts try to guide churches about
leadership structures, church rituals such as baptism and Eucharist, requirements for membership, and the like. Many scholars consider the Pastoral
Epistles part of this genre and date them to early or mid-2nd century, long
after Paul died around 64 CE.

The Pastorals list qualifications for bishops (1 Tim. 3:1–7; Titus 1:7–9),
deacons (1 Tim. 3:8–13), and elders (Titus 1:5–6). They instruct parishioners
to live quiet, pious, undisruptive lives.

In terms of Paul's person, it is difficult to reconcile the apostle Paul who
presents himself like this in Philippians 3:4–6:

If anyone else has reason to be confident in the flesh, I have more:
circumcised on the eighth day, a member of the people of Israel, of
the tribe of Benjamin, a Hebrew born of Hebrews; as to the law, a
Pharisee; as to zeal, a persecutor of the church; as to righteousness
under the law, blameless.

with the author of the Pastorals, who claims:

For we ourselves were once foolish, disobedient, led astray, slaves to
various passions and pleasures, passing our days in malice and envy,
despicable, hating one another. (Titus 3:3)

For all these reasons and more, many scholars do not find suggestions of
Pauline authorship of Colossians, Ephesians, and the Pastorals to be tenable.

---

5. Other examples include the *Didache, Apostolic Constitutions*, and *Didascalia Apostolorum*
(*Teaching of the Twelve Apostles*).

If you want to maintain Pauline authorship of any or all of these texts, you must be prepared to address these issues.

Paul either wrote these texts or he didn't. If Paul did write them, then either (a) he was an extremely inconsistent thinker, or (b) he changed his mind about some of his key theological concepts in a brief period of time. Furthermore, his vocabulary and rhetorical style changed quite dramatically. If that is the case, then one has to decide which Paul is more authoritative: the early Paul who urged women not to marry, or the later Paul who insisted upon it? The early Paul in whose churches women prayed and prophesied and taught (remember Prisca/Priscilla, who instructed Apollos?), or the later Paul who insisted that women shut up and not teach men? Whatever you decide, you must treat all the data before you and not sweep anything under the rug. It's difficult to formulate an argument that leaves no questions, but you will want to make a case that accounts for as much of the data as possible.

If Paul didn't write these texts, certain questions come to the fore.

QUESTIONS RAISED THUS FAR

Let's consider some of the questions that our discussion about biblical authorship of the deuteropauline letters may have raised so far.

1. Why Might Someone Write in Paul's Name? Isn't That Dishonest?

One can view the subject in at least two ways. Positively, there are many examples in antiquity of disciples writing in the name of their teachers. One might consider it to be an act of homage on the part of the disciple who has trained so closely with the master that he or she is certain that "this is what Paul would have said if he had been alive and advising us in these circumstances." It is certainly true that Paul's own letters show that his writing was a team effort. We might want to compare it to the practice of artists who trained as apprentices or in the school of a great master and devoted their lives to perpetuating that master's style throughout their career. When we go to a Rembrandt exhibit, for instance, we see paintings done by his students whose primary goal was to imitate Rembrandt.

Perhaps more negatively, one could accuse the authors of forgery, of being dishonest. If you want your ideas to be accepted and have rhetorical force, however, how much better to write in the name of an authoritative personage? Or perhaps someone wanted to correct certain teachings of Paul and wrote in his name. All are theoretically possible.

2. If Paul Didn't Write These Texts, Who Did?

Scholars offer various suggestions about the authorship of the deuteropauline letters. Some suggest specific individuals, and others keep the identification more general. For instance, Luke is sometimes suggested as the author of the Pastoral Epistles, though most ascribe their authorship more generally to an unknown Gentile Christian writing in the early to mid-2nd century and responding to a number of concerns that had arisen for the church. As noted, Jesus' and Paul's prediction that the Day of the Lord might come during the lifetime of the first generation of Christians did not come to pass. How then might the church be set up to transmit the traditions from generation to generation? How should the church be structured? Upon what basis should leaders be designated? How could the church avoid being persecuted and maligned by the host culture, pagan Gentile neighbors, and the mighty hand of Rome? As the church remained, more and more varieties of Christianity emerged. How could parishioners determine which forms were "true"?

This author clearly considered himself to be a devotee of Paul and, like modern preachers and pastors, was trying his best to adapt the basic teachings of Paul to a new situation, with new problems and concerns with which the apostle himself never had to contend. The same could be said for each of the disputed epistles.

I often hear people ascribe the book of Hebrews to Paul, but unlike the disputed epistles discussed above, the book of Hebrews nowhere claims Pauline authorship. In fact, Hebrews does not take the form of a typical letter that one finds in the Pauline corpus: there's no authorial identification, no identification of the addressees, no greeting. It calls itself an "exhortation," a sermon. It has no proper place in a discussion of Pauline texts.

3. Is It Important to Ponder Whether Paul Wrote Them or Not?

Yes, it really is important. We Christians are a historical people. We believe that God acts within human history in concrete ways. We stand in a tradition that is 2,000 years old; it existed long before us and will probably go on long after you and I are dead. To be faithful to that tradition, we want to understand to the best of our ability its chronological development. We also want to understand its theological development. Theology is always contextual: it is worked out in very specific places and times. It is shaped by the ideas current at the time, and it also shapes the future of the church.

If Paul wrote *both* that women should be church leaders *and* remain silent and have no authority over men, this presents a real interpretive dilemma. If it turns out that those (deuteropauline) letters were written by a later Christian trying to make Christianity succeed under new circumstances, we can perhaps make more sense of the data and thus of how and why our tradition developed as it did. The more we understand the details of our history, the better positioned we are for deciding how best to be a faithful church in our own time.

How we construe Pauline authorship also matters for reconstructing the historical Paul, much as we have to decide which sources to use in constructing the historical Jesus. We want to distinguish the Paul of history from the Paul of the early church as we try to distinguish the Jesus of history and the Christ of faith.

You may argue that the earliest Christians took all of these letters as Pauline and authorship wasn't questioned until 200 years ago. True. Almost nothing about the Bible was questioned until 200 years ago. The Enlightenment started people thinking about all kinds of subjects they'd never considered critically before. For most of Christian history, biblical interpretation was solely in the hands of clergy. Furthermore, you could make the same point about science and medicine. "Well, people always thought Earth was the center of the universe up until Galileo and they did just fine." Would we really want to settle for that view in science? Shouldn't we have at least as high a standard of reflection and pursuit of knowledge with respect to our Scriptures?

4. If Paul Didn't Write Them, Do They Count as Less Authoritative than Paul's Own Writings?

This is a fascinating and complex question, in part because it taps into larger questions of the nature of the canon and scriptural authority. The terms *Bible*, *canon*, and *Scripture* are not synonymous. In Protestant parlance, "the *Bible*" refers to the 39 books found in the Old Testament and the 27 in the New Testament. Catholic and Orthodox Bibles, however, contain books that aren't included in the Protestant Bible.

Canon refers to a defined, restricted list. *Scripture* refers to those texts which a community regards as sacred and authoritative and, typically, inspired. Not all canonical texts function scripturally for Christians. Martin Luther, for instance, had no use for Hebrews, James, Jude, or Revelation and suggested they be excised from the canon. What do you think about his proposal? This leads us to a discussion of the canon.

FORMATION OF THE CHRISTIAN CANON

The Old Testament texts were written over a period of a thousand years, between the 12th and 2nd centuries BCE. The individual books of the New

Testament were composed between 50 and 125 CE by various authors. They were not brought together into the collection of 27 books that we know until hundreds of years after Christ's death. For all of the first followers of Jesus, not to mention Jesus himself, the word "Scripture" refers only to what we call the Old Testament, or Hebrew Bible. So, whenever you see the word "scripture" in the New Testament, it does not include New Testament books. The authors of the New Testament texts used a version of Scripture known as the Septuagint (LXX). The Septuagint includes the Greek translation of the Hebrew Scriptures plus other texts that appear today in Catholic and Orthodox Bibles but are not considered part of the canon by Protestants.

The first Christians wrote many other books besides those that appear in the New Testament today, such as works by the Shepherd of Hermas, *1 Clement* and *2 Clement*, the *Didache*, the letters of Ignatius, the *Acts of Paul and Thecla*, the *Gospel of Mary*, the *Gospel of Peter*, and so on. Like the New Testament books, these texts were used by many ancient churches and shaped their piety and practices. Even the Old Testament canon had not been fully closed by the time of the first Christians. Notice that Jude, for example, quotes both *1 Enoch* and the *Assumption of Moses* as scriptural texts, though they are not considered part of the canon today.

So how and when did we get our present New Testament, which, unlike the Old Testament, is uniform among all Christians?

From Talk to Text

Jesus died around 30 CE. He left nothing in writing. For the next 20 years, his teaching and traditions about him circulated only orally. The church began being church, replete with rituals such as Communion, baptism, catechesis (instructing new converts and those born into the faith), and worship. Materials related to these church practices were the first to be written down. So, within the Epistles, we see evidence of and allusions to liturgical material, hymns, creeds, ritual practices such as baptism and the Lord's Supper, and laying on of hands (1 Cor. 11:23–34; 14:26–33; Jas. 5:13–18; examples of probable hymns include Phil. 2:6–11 and 1 Tim. 3:16). Paul wrote letters in the 50s and then, from 70–100, our Gospels were composed. The latest material in the New Testament was probably written around 125–150 CE.

The texts that made it into the New Testament were used by numerous churches. Paul's Letters were probably the first texts grouped together as churches found that some of his advice to other congregations applied to their own. Other letters were written for multiple congregations in the first place, such as Ephesians and 1 Peter.

Churches were also using many other letters authoritatively that did not make the final canon cut. There were various Gospels, Apocalypses, and Acts that were omitted. Communities had to decide which texts to use in their preaching and teaching, all of which was done communally since most people didn't own books and the literacy level was extremely low. From the very beginning, communities disagreed on which materials were to be used. Let me give you some examples. We have no evidence in the West for James as Scripture before the 4th century; in the East, however, James was already Scripture by the time of Origen (184–254 CE). The Shepherd of Hermas (*Mandates*, *Similitudes*, and *Visions*) was favored by the West and the *Apocalypse of Peter* in the East. Some books were disfavored because of who used them. For instance, an extremely popular movement called the Montanists relied heavily upon Revelation and the Gospel of John, so those books were viewed with suspicion.

By the end of the 2nd century, many of the New Testament books in the canon today were being used scripturally. You may have heard of the Muratorian Fragment, which is tied to Rome and lists books considered canonical by the author of the text, whoever he or she might have been. The list is sometimes dated to the late 2nd century, sometimes to the 4th century. It contains 22 of our 27 books. It's missing 3 John, James, Hebrews, and the Petrine material—strange for a Roman church! It includes the Wisdom of Solomon, and it notes that the *Apocalypse of Peter* and Shepherd of Hermas are regarded highly.

No canon discussion would be complete without mention of *Marcion*. His form of Christianity became hugely popular, and around 150 CE he drew up a list of accepted books. Thus he appears to have been the first to do so. He accepted many letters of Paul and a heavily edited version of Luke. Marcion was a dualist who believed that the visible world is the creation of an evil demiurge; Jesus comes to free humanity from this demiurge's grasp. That demiurge Marcion identified with the Old Testament. Anything associated with Judaism he considers corrupt. Marcion's canon forced the rest of the churches to look at the issue of canon. Marcion was declared a heretic by those religious leaders who would eventually become the guardians of Catholic, orthodox theology.

In his Easter Letter of 367 CE, Bishop Athanasius of Alexandria lists our 27 books and calls them "springs of salvation." The North African Council of Carthage in 397 CE asked for Rome's approval of the list. So, by the close of the 4th century, we have our New Testament. However, not all Christian congregations and individuals agreed with that list or ceased using other books that they had considered authoritative. As mentioned earlier, Luther himself challenged the canon, especially Hebrews, James, Jude, and

Revelation. The Council of Trent (1546) reaffirmed the 27 books, as did the Articles of the Church of England (1562/1571) and the Westminster Confession (1647).

So, the formation of the Christian canon involved a long, gradual process. At the end of the day, books that made it into the New Testament canon did so largely on the basis of three criteria taken together: use, apostolicity, and some notion of a "rule of faith."

Use

Various churches in different geographical locations found the texts useful for worship and spiritual formation. This criterion alone was not decisive, however, since the *Didache* and the Shepherd of Hermas were surely used more widely than, say, Jude; yet neither made it into the canon while Jude did.

Apostolicity

If a writing were somehow shown to derive from an apostle, its chances for inclusion in the canon increased. While none of our canonical Gospels ever identify their authors, Matthew and John eventually were tied to the apostles Matthew and John. What about Mark and Luke, neither of whom were apostles? Their authority was bolstered by connecting them to apostles indirectly. For instance, the Gospel of Mark becomes associated with the apostle Peter such that Peter's companion Mark became his secretary or translator. The Gospel of Luke gets connected to the apostle Paul such that Paul's companion Luke conveys something of Paul through his composition of Luke/Acts.

Associating a text with a particular apostle was not always a decisive factor for its inclusion, however. If it had been, then the *Gospel of Peter*, the *Apocalypse of Peter*, the *Gospel of Philip*, the *Acts of Paul and Thecla*, and many other texts used and beloved by faithful early Christians would have been included.[6]

"Rule of Faith" (*Regula Fidei*)

As the church became more institutionalized and centralized, notions of orthodoxy and heresy developed. A genre of literature arose called *against heresies*. Sacred texts that adhered to what was deemed to be orthodox by the church leadership had a better chance than those whose theology appeared

---

6. Neither was age of the text the criterion for inclusion, since 2 Peter, which eventually made it, was probably written later than both *1 Clement* or the *Didache*, which didn't.

heretical or those associated with groups whose theology and practice were designated heretical. So, the Gospel of John, loved by gnostics almost to a person, had suspicion cast upon it. Some books that do not appear to offend orthodoxy, such as the *Didache* and the Shepherd of Hermas, nonetheless didn't make the canon cut.

Therefore, no one criterion was enough to ensure inclusion. Different texts had their champions and their detractors. The process was complex and not always clear. Luke Johnson makes this provocative comment:

> It has been asserted in the past, and more urgently in the present, that the process of canonization was one that was inherently corrupt. According to this view, entirely worthy writings of diverse forms of Christian life were ruthlessly suppressed by orthodox leaders out of unworthy motives. Because of this, the whole issue of the canon ought to be opened again, with all the writings produced by earliest Christianity given an equal weighting as this generation decides what its Bible ought to be. According to this argument, the important stage of canonization was that of ratification by bishops. These bishops were politically motivated, and conditioned as well by the cultural attitudes of their day. In every decision, they chose that which was conservative over that which was radical; chose institution rather than charisma; fought for hierarchy rather than egalitarianism; preferred doctrine to mysticism; suppressed women in favor of men. The canon we now have, therefore, is not the canon of the whole church, but only of a victorious segment of the church.[7]

How does such a statement strike you the reader? Why?

CANON AND SCRIPTURAL AUTHORITY

For us to answer the question of how these texts function authoritatively for us, we have to ask why we read the texts. What are we looking for there? What do we expect to find?

There are different *reasons* to read Scripture, and there are different *ways* to read it. Christians expect to meet Christ there. And I use the word "meet" on purpose there, in all its senses. I mean it in the sense of being introduced to someone new. I mean it in the sense of a routine gathering as in staff meetings, an ongoing checking in with one another to keep the lines of communication open. And I mean it in the sense of being met, of someone waiting for you, looking for you, being ready for your arrival.

---

7. Luke Timothy Johnson, *The Writings of the New Testament: An Interpretation* (Philadelphia: Fortress Press, 1986), 542–43.

We read for *historical* purposes. What was it like to be an ancient believer? How did the Christian tradition develop over time?

We read for *ethical* insight. What would God have us do? How do we know what is good and what is not? Think about the Sermon on the Mount. Using the Bible in ethical decision making is not always as straightforward as one might think since at some points the Bible reflects and supports practices that modern Christians would find unethical, such as slavery. Furthermore, sometimes we turn to the Bible to argue for a certain position on a contemporary issue that the Bible might not specifically address, such as abortion, gun control, birth control, or ordaining gay or lesbian people. Often people seem to have their mind made up before turning to Scripture and pull from it those verses that appear to support their preconceived view; people with completely opposing stances claim that Scripture validates their own position.

Further, some issues are no longer live for most us, such as whether or not it is proper for a Christian to consume meat sacrificed to idols. In this case you might want to argue for the "general idea" conveyed in the biblical situation and dismiss the specific issue. How do you decide, though, when to be specific and when not to be? Some folks want to get specific about not getting drunk, but seem to ignore the Pastorals' prohibition against jewelry and braided hair. Are we bound by the ethics of the New Testament?

So, is Scripture an ethical guide? Consider this statement by a famous sociologist of religion: "In an otherwise secular society the church must in fact be different. It must do strange things to provide a place where the voice of God can at least be imagined, if not actually heard. Clergy do well when they make outrageous statements about love and forgiveness, and congregants do well when they make the even more outrageous attempt to put these statements into practice."[8] Scripture certainly helps us as we explore and determine how we might best conduct ourselves, but it probably works best when it is engaged in a studious, nuanced, informed manner.[9]

Some people appeal to Scripture to form a *systematic theology*. The New Testament itself does not contain a systematic theology, but it can serve as a resource for those trying to construct one. It testifies to the diversity of the early church as those first Christians sought to work out their faith in the real world. Paul does not write treatises "On God" or "On Humanity." He says, "Hey, I hear some of you have stopped sleeping with your spouses. Hey, I hear some of you are sleeping with prostitutes. Hey, I hear some of you think

---

8. Robert Wuthnow, *Producing the Sacred: An Essay on Public Religion* (Champaign: University of Illinois Press, 1994), 58.

9. For a useful book on using Scripture in ethical considerations, read Charles H. Cosgrove, *Appealing to Scripture in Moral Debate: Five Hermeneutical Rules* (Grand Rapids: Wm. B. Eerdmans Pub. Co., 2002).

you're better than others because you're richer, smarter, and more power-ful." These are glimpses in other times of people somewhat like us, somewhat different from us, working out their particular joys and problems in a certain place in a certain time. The apostle Paul, also constrained in part by human finitude, does the best he can with what he's got (according to his own words in 1 Cor. 7, e.g., 7:6, 12, 25, 40).

Scripture also functions the way *great literature* does. Listen to these words from Tobias Wolff, introducing a collection of short stories—what he says about their power applies equally to Scripture: "That sense of kinship is what makes stories important to us. The pleasure we take in cleverness and techni-cal virtuosity soon exhausts itself in the absence of any recognizable human landscape. We need to feel ourselves acted upon by a story, outraged, exposed, in danger of heartbreak and change. Those are the stories that endure in our memories, to the point where they take on the nature of memory itself. In this way the experience of something read can form us no less than the experience of something lived through."[10] Can you think of stories in Scripture that have affected you deeply in some way? Which ones? Why?

Scripture also serves the church *liturgically*. It shapes the way we conduct worship. As one person observed: "When you join Rotary they give you a handshake and a lapel pin. When you join the church we throw you in the water and half drown you. Ponder that. Whatever signing on with Jesus means, it means that we will not do just as we are, that change is demanded, daily, sometimes painful turning and detoxification that does not come naturally."[11] "In baptism we are taught to find our strength in God and God's people rather than ourselves. We are prepared for the shock of moral transformation by a cleansing, cold bath. We are born, drowned, adopted, clothed, gifted so that we might be a people worthy of listening to a peculiar account of human life called Scripture."[12]

In some ways Scripture seems familiar and timeless. Many of the problems the biblical figures face we also experience, for better or worse. But much about our world is different from theirs. At every turn, Christians are able to read these texts and ponder the convergences and divergences of our experi-ence and knowledge with that of our ancient forebears. From there the mod-ern church must decide what it all means for us in this time and in this place. Different churches decide differently.

---

10. Tobias Wolff, *The Vintage Book of American Short Stories* (New York: Vintage Contem-poraries, 1994), xiii.

11. William Willimon, *Peculiar Speech: Preaching to the Baptized* (Grand Rapids: Wm. B. Eerd-mans Pub. Co., 1992), 32.

12. Ibid., 22.

Many churches and individual Christians operate according to a "canon within the canon," whether or not they know it or admit it. Which texts and doctrines get the most attention in your church? Why? If you were asked to pick the texts that convey the essence of your faith and convictions, which would you list? Why? Protestants, thanks to Luther, tend to rely heavily upon Paul to articulate their theology, especially his view of justification by faith through grace.

How does Pauline authorship and scriptural authority fit in? Take the issue of women's ordination. If you belong to a church that opposes women's ordination, you will probably hear an argument like the following:

> The apostle Paul wrote 1 Timothy, which clearly states that women can have no authority over men. Therefore, they cannot hold leadership positions in church. Furthermore, Paul wrote in Ephesians 5 that wives must submit to their husbands and that husbands are the spiritual head of the household. So, in both the church and the home, God has ordained men to rule and lead while women are to submit to that male leadership.

For example, the resolution from the Southern Baptist Convention in 1984 stripping women of the right of ordination reads as follows (note that all of the references are taken from the Pastoral Epistles):

> WHEREAS, while Paul commends women and men alike in other roles of ministry and service (Titus 2:1–10) he excludes women from pastoral leadership (I Timothy 2:12) to preserve a submission God requires because the man was first in Creation and the woman was first in the Edenic fall (I Timothy 2:13ff.).[13]

Such churches tend to claim that the Bible alone is the single authoritative source for doctrine and polity. Read Titus 2:1–10, which is cited above. Note that it also says, "Tell slaves to be submissive to their masters and to give satisfaction in every respect. . . ." Now, to be consistent, I assume that those who oppose women's ordination on the basis of the Pastoral Epistles must also believe that those who find themselves enslaved (as many human beings are as I write this since human trafficking is a vibrant trade) should obey those currently enslaving them, and the church should promote such relationships. Whenever I present this argument, I usually hear something about how the texts concerning slavery are time-constrained and we don't believe in that kind of treatment of people anymore. Then how can you readily adopt the ancient standards on gender? It's inconsistent. Furthermore, the Pastoral Epistles speak of qualifications for bishops, deacons, and elders. Southern

13. See http://www.womenpriests.org/related/sbaptist.asp#1984.

Baptists do not have bishops and elders. Why not? The very same texts used to forbid women's ordination expect bishops and elders. Again, it's a serious inconsistency on the part of those who claim to follow the Bible literally. To adopt the standards on gender but not on church offices and slavery treated in the very same texts—that is quite problematic logically.

If, on the other hand, you belong to a church that supports women's ordination, you will hear something like this:

> Paul's preaching and ministry in the undisputed letters make clear that he supports both women and men in leadership roles. Paul expected the world to end at any moment so he did not lay down directives for setting up the church as an enduring institution with particular offices like bishop, elder, and so forth. He died in 64 CE. Jesus did not return. The church then began to hunker down for the long haul. As it became institutionalized, it abandoned the egalitarian, countercultural vision of both Jesus and Paul and instead adopted the hierarchical structures regnant in the host culture, the Roman Empire. The household codes of Colossians and Ephesians simply adopt Greek philosophical concepts of gender, household structure, and political structures. These texts were not, in fact, written by Paul but by later devotees trying to interpret Paul for their own time. These texts are authoritative in that they are not to be ignored; they must be addressed and studied and understood. Much in these texts continues to manifest good news to the world today powerfully. Those parts that reflect the adoption of the host culture's oppressive structures are not binding on the church today, but they do call the church (a) to repentance for selling out to categories determined by pagan culture for so long and (b) to watchfulness lest we do the same in our own time and culture.
>
> Such churches as this readily recognize and articulate that Scripture is one authority for the church, but not the sole authority. The church also appeals to reason (created and informed by God as attested by the wisdom tradition) and experience.

When We Say That the Bible Is Authoritative, What Do We Mean?

At the very least we mean that it shapes our identity as God's people who everywhere and at all times proclaim the redemption and hope wrought by God through the work of Jesus Christ, God's Word made flesh. We mean that these texts, more than any others, have stood the test of time for encouraging, challenging, and transforming Christians. Though we often enjoy study groups at church that discuss some nonbiblical text or book of the day, when we congregate for worship of God, it is these biblical texts that we gather around for worship. When we commit to passing the tradition on to our youth and new members, we pass on these texts, generation after generation after generation. When we celebrate the birth of someone or something new, when we exult in our transcendent, ecstatic experiences, these texts give us true, solid, substantial language to express them. When we bury our loved ones and our dreams, when we mourn losses great and small, these texts provide words to express our rage, desolation, confusion, and yes, our hope. The authority of Scripture may mean far more than this, but it certainly means no less.

What about Other Books of the Bible?

In this chapter we have focused on authorship issues related to the Pauline corpus. Though we raised the issue of authorship briefly when discussing the Synoptic Problem, they are not identical situations. No Gospel mentions who wrote it. The books we have come to label Matthew, Mark, Luke, and John do not claim to have been written by Matthew, Mark, Luke, and John. But Colossians, Ephesians, 1 and 2 Timothy, and Titus do claim to have been written by the Paul who wrote the seven undisputed epistles.

What about the other books?

James claims to be written by "James, a servant of God and of the Lord Jesus Christ." The author tells us nothing else about himself. As is the case today, James was a common name at that time. Who is this James? It's difficult to know because a number of persons are called James in the New Testament. They are usually dubbed James the Just (Jesus' brother but not one of the twelve apostles), James the Less, and James the Great (one of Zebedee's sons, brother of John). These three are then variously conflated (it's much like trying to sort out all the Marys in the NT). If it was written by Jesus' brother, it's odd that he doesn't mention that he is Jesus' brother. It's also puzzling why he doesn't mention Jesus and his teachings. In fact, he only mentions Jesus twice, once in 1:1, which I quoted above, and once in 2:1, in reference again to "Lord Jesus Christ." Some scholars argue that this was originally a Jewish document taken over by Christians who "Christianized" it by adding the word "Jesus" a couple of times. It is considered part of the Wisdom literature of the Bible, kin to Proverbs, Job, and Ecclesiastes. For his part, Martin Luther dubbed it "a right strawy epistle which does not show thee Christ."[14]

Jude is a rather odd little book that claims to be written by "Jude, a servant of Jesus Christ and brother of James." Some take this to mean that the James

14. Martin Luther in September 1522, in the preface to his New Testament in German; in *Luther's Works*, ed. J. Pelikan and H. T. Lehmann, 55 vols. (St. Louis: Concordia; Philadelphia: Fortress Press, 1955–86), 35:362.

mentioned here is the brother of Jesus, which would make the author also a brother of Jesus. If so, why does the author not clarify this? Those who consider it written by a brother of Jesus date it to 60–90. Those who consider it pseudonymous date it to the first part of the 2nd century. Recall that Bishop Eusebius lists it as "disputed" even in the 4th century.

1 John does not mention its author by name so one must use evidence external to the text to make an argument for authorship. Tradition claims that it was written by the apostle John; it also claims that the same John wrote the Gospel of John. Recall, however, that the Gospel of John does not name its author. The authorship debate gets somewhat complicated since (a) the letter never claims to be written by anyone named John; and (b) once one suggests "John" as its author, one has to argue for the various Johns of tradition.

2 and 3 John claim to be written by "the elder" (Greek: *presbyteros*). The author provides no other identifying information, so it is difficult to discern who wrote them. Tradition calls the author John the Presbyter to distinguish him from the author of 1 John, the Gospel of John, and Revelation.

Unlike the Gospel of John, 1 John, 2 John, and 3 John, the book of Revelation *does* claim to be authored by someone named John! "I, John, your brother who shares with you in Jesus the persecution and the kingdom and the patient endurance, was on the island called Patmos because of the word of God and the testimony of Jesus" (1:9). This John is referred to, then, as John of Patmos. Beyond this identification, the author does not mention having written any other texts, so it's difficult to discern who this John is since, like today, it was a common name. John the Apostle, John the Evangelist (the traditional author of the Fourth Gospel), and John of Patmos are considered three distinct people by many; others combine them in various ways.

2 Peter claims to be written by the apostle Peter, but the vast majority of biblical scholars consider it to be pseudepigraphical, in no way written by the apostle.

1 Peter claims to be written by "Peter, an apostle of Jesus Christ" (1:1). If so, it was written in the early 60s. But the authorship of 1 Peter is hotly contested on a number of counts. I belong to an online Bible study group called Ecclesia, run by Dr. Carolyn J. Sharp, Associate Professor of Hebrew Scriptures at Yale Divinity School, who provides wonderful brief studies and open discussion about one book of the Bible at a time. During the study of 1 Peter, Dr. Sharp wrote the following:

> Many scholars think this letter was not really written by Simon Peter, the disciple of Jesus. Why? Four main reasons:
> 1. The letter seems to reflect circumstances in Asia Minor that were later than Peter could have lived unless he was really, really old.

2. 1 Peter is written in a kind of Greek that is stylistically polished. This would make it unlikely that Peter wrote it himself, since he is called an "uneducated and ordinary" man in Acts 4:13. (We might object, here, that the description in Acts 4 might be for *rhetorical* purposes, to make it all the more astounding that Peter and John could testify so eloquently; so maybe Peter was not so uneducated after all, . . . but in any case, there is an issue here.)

3. When the letter quotes Scripture, it is quoting the Septuagint—the ancient Greek translation of the Hebrew Scriptures—rather than the Hebrew original. As with # 2 above, this seems a somewhat unlikely capability for Peter as he is described in the Gospels and Acts.

4. The letter does not mention things in Jesus's life that Peter would have seen. Some scholars argue that the absence of personal reminiscences about Jesus would be unlikely if the author really had been Peter. (I think this argument is weak, myself.)

> Scholar Paul Achtemeier says that the author of 1 Peter probably had enjoyed some level of formal education; if not an "advanced" education in rhetoric or philosophy, at least a "middle" education that would have included, along with geometry, arithmetic, and music, a reading of such classical authors as Homer. While one may surely presume some facility in Greek even among Palestinian fishermen in the first century who lacked formal education, the kind of Greek found in this epistle was probably beyond such a person.[15]

Other scholars have responded that even if Peter was initially unlettered, he would have improved his language skills in order to carry out his Christian mission more effectively.

> One way or another, don't let this authorship question threaten your faith. You may certainly believe the historical Peter wrote it; or you may find it just as sacred, just as revelatory, even if the author was someone else who was *drawing on the identity of Peter* to make a particular point. To me, what matters is that it's in sacred Scripture. It's a beautiful, stirring letter, and it's a gift from God. I find it wonderful to imagine the historical Peter writing it, even though I acknowledge that there are problems with that authorship. (emphasis added)[16]

What is your reaction to Dr. Sharp's presentation? Do you think it matters whether or not Peter wrote 1 Peter? Why or why not? How does your answer relate to your estimation of the Pauline material?

There is no doubt that your decisions about authorship affect how you reconstruct the chronological and doctrinal development of the church from

15. Paul Achtemeier, *1 Peter* (Minneapolis: Fortress Press, 1996), 4–5.

16. Quoted with permission, from "Ecclesia—an Ongoing Forum for Scripture Study," running since 2006: http://mailman.yale.edu/mailman/listinfo/ecclesia. This section is from the June 1, 2009, posting.

a historical perspective. What other effects rest upon how one understands biblical authorship? If one looks under "Pseudepigraph" in Wikipedia, one reads the following, which I find eminently germane to our present discussion:

> Pseudepigrapha . . . are falsely attributed works, texts whose claimed authorship is unfounded; a work, simply, "whose real author attributed it to a figure of the past." For instance, no Hebrew scholars would ascribe the book of Enoch to Enoch, a character mentioned in Genesis 5, and few liberal Christian scholars would insist today that the Second Epistle of Peter was written by Saint Peter. *Nevertheless, in some cases, especially for books belonging to a religious canon, the question of whether a text is pseudepigraphical or not elicits sensations of loyalty and can become a matter of heavy dispute. The authenticity or value of the work itself, which is a separate question for experienced readers, often becomes sentimentally entangled in the association.* Though the inherent value of the text may not be called into question, the weight of a revered or even apostolic author lends authority to a text. In antiquity pseudepigraphy was "an accepted and honored custom practiced by students/admirers of a revered figure." This is the essential motivation for pseudepigraphy. (emphasis added)

Do you think, as the above author does, that the value of a work is separate from the issue of authentic authorship?

Sometimes as I host discussions on these matters, I hear the question, "Can I trust the Bible if Paul didn't write Colossians and Peter didn't write 2 Peter?" I will not presume to answer that question for you, dear reader, but I would ask, "Trust the Bible to do what? To be what? Upon what or whom is your own faith based?" As my former professor David Bartlett says, "We are a Jesus-believing people who have the Bible, not a Bible-believing people who have Jesus." I suspect that this statement emerged from his study of Karl Barth, who contended that the Bible was the word of God insofar as it points to the Word of God, Jesus. But others will disagree. What do you think?

Whatever you and your church decide, consider these words of the rabbis about Scripture: "Turn it and turn it again, for everything is in it; and contemplate it and grow grey and old over it and stir not from it" (Mishnah *Avot* 5:22)

STUDY QUESTIONS

1. What questions or issues does this chapter raise for you?
2. Which books are included in the Bible that your church uses?
3. What position does your church take on biblical authorship?

4. In what way(s) does your church consider Scripture to be authoritative?
5. In what way(s) do you personally consider Scripture to be authoritative?
6. Do you think it's helpful that we have a closed canon, or do you think it should be reopened for discussion? Are there parts that should be omitted? Are there texts from beyond the 2nd century that should be added? What if tomorrow we discovered another authentic Pauline letter—should we add it? Give explanations for your answers.

6

The Historical Jesus Debate

The historical Jesus debate never fails to engage the seminarians, clergy, and laity whom I teach. Emotions run high and opinions are strong. The debate among scholars has modeled intemperate, supercilious vitriol. Even the late Raymond Brown, renowned for his meticulous, moderate treatments of academic issues, succumbs to the temptation in his *An Introduction to the New Testament*, in the chapter on the historical Jesus. Luke Johnson does the same in *The Real Jesus*. Both of those scholars lambaste the Jesus Seminar. One student approached me to share that she was so outraged after reading her historical Jesus assignment (drawn from Mark Allen Powell's *Jesus as a Figure in History*, hardly an extremist presentation of the debate, and David Barr's *New Testament Story: An Introduction*) that she had called her pastor in distress. My comment during the class that evening, however—noting that a former student had confided in me that if it weren't for the historical Jesus conversation, he would not still be in the church or in seminary—made her reconsider her outrage.

What is "the Quest for the historical Jesus"? Why does it elicit such strong reactions from all parties? Why are some Christians disgusted by it and afraid of it while others are moved to a deeper faith? What difference does the historical Jesus make to the New Testament authors and the life of the church? To what extent does Christian identity depend upon the historical Jesus? If the names Marcus Borg, John Dominic Crossan, or Robert Funk mean nothing to you, then you probably have not been captivated by the historical Jesus debate. What's it all about?

We've devoted a lot of time thus far to the apostle Paul (who wrote in the 50s) and to the Gospel writers, who wrote about Jesus from 70 to 100 CE. But have you ever wondered about the flesh-and-blood human being Jesus of

Nazareth who was an actual historical personage like you and me? Who was born around 4 BCE and died around 33 CE? Who lived at a particular historical moment in a certain geographical locale in a particular cultural, political, economic, social environment, with parents and siblings and presuppositions as a Jewish man living in Galilee in the 1st century? Many of us Christians think of Jesus only in terms of his divinity, his role as cocreator of the universe and Savior of humankind. But if the incarnation is to be taken seriously, that is, if God really does act in human history in very particular ways, then should we not concern ourselves with the historical human aspects of Jesus? You and I are certainly finite beings born into particular social, political, economic circumstances that shape our thoughts and goals and our sense of who we are vis-à-vis the world into which we are born. If Jesus was fully human, what kind of human would he have been in the 1st century in Galilee under Roman rule? The historical Jesus, then, refers to the Jesus we can reconstruct by using historical methods.

I don't know if you've seen Mel Gibson's movie *The Passion of the Christ*, but one thing that struck me in it was Jesus' multilingual abilities. When speaking to his countrymen, he orates in Aramaic; but when speaking to Pilate, he facilely switches into Latin. I was flummoxed on two counts: first, nowhere do the Gospels depict Jesus as a purveyor of Latin; second, it is quite unlikely that a carpenter from Galilee in the 1st century would have any facility with Latin. When I asked a friend from a very conservative tradition about this discrepancy, she explained that Jesus, as God, would have known all of the world's languages!

Long ago, a helpful distinction was made: "the Jesus of history and the Christ of faith." What's the difference between the two? Jesus of Nazareth was a historical personage who was born, lived, and died within a particular time and place. He was, first and foremost, a practicing Jew living in a country occupied by a foreign political power, Rome. He was crucified by Rome around 33 CE. For all the influence and power that his life and death have had upon subsequent history, his life and death had little impact on the early historical literary record. He left nothing in writing, and he appears only rarely in non-Christian materials.

On the other hand, much attention has been devoted to the "Christ of faith." Christ (Greek: *Christos*), of course, is not an actual name; it's the title for an office, means "the anointed," and is a Greek translation of Hebrew *mashiakh*, from which we derive the term "messiah." So, *messiah* and *christ* are synonyms in two different languages simply meaning "anointed." Readers of the Old Testament are quite familiar with the practice of anointing whereby a leader of the people is designated by God, often through the hands of a prophet. So Christ represents a kind of office, perhaps as we would say "Mother Anna" for a nun or "Father Tom" for a priest or "Senator so-and-so." Christ is a *title* that represents an office with a long-established tradition of meaning and function. Kings, such as King David, were certainly anointed and called to carry out the work of the God of Israel.

Christians believe that Jesus of Nazareth also was anointed and acted in the role of God's anointed to carry out God's plan for redemption and salvation. This was accomplished, according to Christian doctrine, by the cross and resurrection of Jesus the Christ. But such claims are matters of faith and go beyond the parameters of history as an academic subject.

If it's useful to distinguish between the Jesus of history and the Christ of faith, it's equally important to distinguish between the Jesus movement and the early church. Technically (and sociologically) speaking, the Jesus Movement is coterminous with the historical Jesus and refers to the activity of Jesus of Nazareth and his followers through the period of Jesus' crucifixion. At that point, the historical Jesus is dead, and history as a field of inquiry cannot comment about Jesus' existence beyond the point of death. It can comment only on what people *believed* (or continue to believe) about Jesus' existence beyond the point of death. At the moment when Jesus' followers declared themselves to have experienced Jesus of Nazareth raised from the dead and placing a call upon them and their lives, you have the end of the Jesus Movement and the beginning of what will come to be called "Christianity." The birth of the church is predicated upon the resurrection of Jesus of Nazareth, regardless of how one construes the doctrine of resurrection. Jesus' resurrection is a matter of proclamation, faith, and experience: it thus falls outside the purview of history's methods and admissible data.

THE FIRST QUEST

Interest in Jesus as the subject of historical inquiry first arose during the Enlightenment period, when the fruits of disinterested, objective inquiry were being sought in the realm of science; it was only a matter of time before the spotlight turned to religious subjects, including Jesus. Scholars began to study the Bible as a historical document alongside other historical documents. Reason and Science loomed large as masters who must be served. Nearly all histories of the quest begin with Hermann Reimarus (1694–1768), who composed 4,000 pages addressing the historical Jesus issue. He didn't publish them in his own lifetime since to do so would have meant social and professional suicide. Posthumously, his works were circulated by Gerhard Lessing.

Reimarus was perhaps the first to draw a distinction between the message of Jesus and that of his disciples. Jesus, he discerned, saw himself as an anointed political leader whose vision of the kingdom of God meant an imminent end to Roman rule. After Jesus was crucified by Rome, which continued to rule mightily, the disciples, rather than admit failure and defeat, "likely stole Jesus' body from the tomb . . . and invented the message of his atoning death and return in glory."[1]

D. F. Strauss's *Life of Jesus* marks the next watershed moment in the Quest. First published in 1835–36, it cost him dearly both personally and professionally. He was fired from his academic post and became a social pariah. But much of what Strauss proposed wouldn't cause the batting of an eyelash today among many faithful Christians. Strauss taught us that we need not be prisoners of literal, historical categories but instead we can explore the mythological aspects of the faith. That is, he taught us to see the Gospels as stories that convey deep truths and draw upon the imagination and nonprosaic facets of human language. He critiqued the "rationalist" approach, which tried to subject all the data to scientific, rationalist categories. Where the rationalists "explained" the miracle of the loaves and fishes not as a supernatural event, but rather as an instance where Jesus inspired people to share with one another the extra goods they had been holding back in their lunch-boxes, Strauss wanted to look at the deeper meaning indicated by such a story.

The main contribution of the early Questers was to force Christians to take history and reason seriously. They taught us to view the Gospels individually and be honest about the discrepancies that are found therein with respect to chronology, verbiage, and depictions of Jesus' life and death. What sources did these early Questers employ? They used the canonical Gospels. After noting the discrepancies, their next task was to rank the importance of each Gospel with respect to historical accuracy. Mark quickly became the favorite since it's the shortest and appears most rudimentary in terms of language and style. Matthew and Luke are much more sophisticated and developed and, therefore, must be later. The Gospel of John was omitted from the outset of the Quest since John was seen to be entirely theological rather than historical, as if the two were contradictory terms. Reader, please beware of such false dichotomies!

This "scholarly consensus" (reader, please beware of "scholarly consensuses"!) regarding Mark's literal, historical veracity was shattered in 1901 by William Wrede's book, *The Messianic Secret*. In it, he demonstrated that Mark is just as "theologically" driven as any other Gospel.

1. David B. Gowler, *What Are They Saying about the Historical Jesus?* (New York: Paulist Press, 2007), 4.

JESUS: APOCALYPTIC OR NOT?

In addition to new questions about the nature of the Gospel materials, questions were raised about Jesus' own religious convictions. Obviously, Jesus was a Jew. But as it turns out, many types of Judaism were at play in Jesus' own time, just as there are many types of Christianity in circulation today, some of which are almost mutually exclusive. One major debate that you will find among Questers has to do with Jesus' apocalyptic views. Did Jesus think the world would end very soon, within his own lifetime? Or was he more of a liberal humanist who raised deeply existential questions about the nature of human beings and how they might best coexist as authentic, enlightened folk? Or is this a false dichotomy altogether?

The issue was raised mightily by Albert Schweitzer in his famous book *The Quest of the Historical Jesus*, first published in 1906. Whereas the previous Questers had painted a (German) sometimes Enlightened, sometimes romantic Jesus who had universal ethical maxims in mind and was an individual virtuoso akin to a Mozart or Beethoven, and who would have easily held forth in high German society, Schweitzer placed Jesus squarely in dusty, occupied Palestine many centuries earlier. For Schweitzer, Jesus was an apocalyptic thinker who determined that God would act immediately in a decisive, cataclysmic fashion and that such a scenario was dependent upon his own choice to suffer. Jesus was wrong, however. The end did not come, despite his best efforts. As Schweitzer famously wrote:

> Jesus . . . in the knowledge that he is the coming Son of Man lays hold of the wheel of the world to set it moving on that last revolution which is to bring all ordinary history to a close. It refuses to turn, and He throws Himself on it. Then it does turn; and crushes Him. Instead of bringing in the eschatological conditions, He has destroyed them. The wheel rolls onward, and the mangled body of the one immeasurably great Man, who was strong enough to think of Himself as the spiritual ruler of mankind and to bend history to His purpose, is hanging upon it still. That is His victory and His reign.

Schweitzer's contributions to our thinking are enormous. First, he reminds us all of what should be obvious: Jesus was not an Enlightenment German philosopher or modern American Democrat or Republican, for that matter. He was a Jew from the artisan class in 1st-century Palestine. He is not to be domesticated and squished into our tidy, modern, comfortable categories. Jesus is, in some ways, extremely foreign to us. If he was an urgent apocalyptist (like a David Koresh) rather than a philosophical sage (like a Deepak Chopra or the Dalai Lama) or self-help guru (à la Dr. Phil), then he's on the weirder side for most modern Americans.

The result of the first Quest was, for the most part, to indicate that the historical Jesus who slept, woke, ate, drank, became ill, bathed (or not), loved, dreamed, despaired, laughed, cried, and died was almost impossible to recover using the tools of history. What mattered about Jesus was his history-of-effects, his ethic of love, or some such abstraction that could serve as a guiding principle for moderns so far removed from 1st-century Palestine.

THE NEW QUEST

Schweitzer's work effectively stymied the flow of historical Jesus research for half a century. Rudolf Bultmann was the next great figure in the debate insofar as he declared that the historical Jesus is not particularly relevant to Christian faith. People do not come to faith on the basis of knowing the historical details of Jesus of Nazareth's life. It's the risen Christ proclaimed in the church's preaching and teaching that addresses human beings directly and transformationally. The resurrection cannot be proved via historical means; it's a matter of faith. The real questions are these: When you are presented with the gospel of Christ as proclaimed by the church, do you feel confronted or addressed in any personal way? Does it make you take stock of the meaning of your life and your purpose on this earth? Do you sense God calling you to a deeper, richer, more authentic existence? That is the Jesus who matters, who effects palpable change in the lives of individuals and communities.

Bultmann sought to "demythologize" the New Testament, to ferret out the basic universal kernels of wisdom embedded in ancient forms so foreign to moderns, such as miracles. In so doing, Bultmann moved readers beyond the impasse created by Schweitzer—that is, Bultmann dug through the "sediment" of the ancient material to pull out the "nuggets" relevant and urgent for his own era. On the down side, he, like those before him, created Jesus in his own image, this time as an existential Western philosopher of the 20th century. He entirely dispensed with that enigmatic, possibly hirsute, earthy craftsman of the 1st century.

Enter Ernst Käsemann, a student of Bultmann's who contested his teacher by insisting that the Jesus of history *does* matter for Christians and their faith. There must be some direct connection between Jesus the man from Nazareth and Christ the risen Lord, or our faith is in vain. It's not valid for Christians to totally disregard the Jesus of history. Käsemann, then, is considered the founder of the New Quest, which occurred in the 1950s. It sought to counter Bultmann's apparent dismissal of the importance of the historical Jesus and to demonstrate the continuity between the Jesus of history and the Christ of faith. But how was one to determine where the Jesus of history ends and the Christ of faith begins? Was Jesus of Nazareth born in Nazareth or Bethlehem? Did he fancy himself a prophet, the Son of Man, a Messiah, God, some or all of the above? What counts as evidence in such debates? What methods are available to help us distinguish between what the historical Jesus, a Jew of the 1st century, would have believed and taught, and what the Christ of faith, product of the Christian church, would have taught? Scholars began developing criteria for sorting out the two.

One is the *criterion of dissimilarity*. This criterion insists that anything that puts Jesus at odds with traditional Judaism is more likely to be authentic. If he was just saying the same old stuff, he wouldn't have caused such upheaval and garnered such disrespect from the Jewish authorities. The problem with this criterion is at least twofold. First, it assumes that Judaism in Jesus' day was uniform, but we have come to understand that this is a false picture. Judaism was quite varied in Jesus' day. Second, it pits Jesus against his own religious tradition. To count only places where Jesus goes *against* Judaism is to disregard the fact that he considered himself a Jew, as did everyone else, including Pilate, who crucified him. It makes no sense whatsoever to posit a non-Jewish Jesus.

The other aspect of the criterion of dissimilarity to consider is this: the items that patently distinguish Jesus from the teachings of the early church are more likely to be authentic since, over time, the church would mold the Jesus of history to its own agenda. It is useful to ask, as a corrective, where the church in antiquity and presently has parted ways with Jesus of Nazareth. But to countenance only those sayings of Jesus which make him sound "undomesticated" by the later church is to suggest complete discontinuity between Jesus and the faith that grew up around him. That's rather extreme and perhaps absurd.

At any rate, the New Quest forced us into the question of how we could best proceed methodologically to arrive at a conclusion that had some cachet as history.

THE THIRD QUEST

The Jesus Seminar

The Third Quest began in the 1980s, continues into the present, and is marked by considerable diversity. This is when the Jesus Seminar, under the leadership of Robert Funk and John Dominic Crossan, began to meet and debate about which words and deeds of Jesus ascribed to him in ancient sources were likely to have stemmed from the historical Jesus himself. Famously, these 30 scholars used a system of colored beads to register their votes:

- *Red* if Jesus said it
- *Pink* if Jesus probably said something like it though it got reworded in the transmission process
- *Gray* if Jesus didn't actually say these words but they somehow accord with his ideas
- *Black* if Jesus definitely didn't say it. Rather, these materials reflect the convictions of the early church which formed after Jesus' death.

They have published their results in *The Five Gospels* and *The Acts of Jesus*.[2] Individual members have also published their own books on the historical Jesus. *The Five Gospels* translates the four canonical Gospels plus the *Gospel of Thomas* and uses the above color-coded system to render judgment on which traditions go all the way back to Jesus. The Seminar is particularly fond of Q and tends to privilege Q and the *Gospel of Thomas* as sources usually more authoritative than the canonical Gospels. We discussed Q in a previous chapter devoted to the Synoptic Problem. At its most basic, Q refers to the verses shared by Matthew and Luke but absent in Mark. The material consists of sayings of Jesus. Numerous scholars go much further, however, and posit a community that had Q as its primary Gospel. They try to reconstruct the historical development and layers of this "Q community" along with its theology. The Jesus Seminar scholars take the Q community very seriously. Others doubt even the existence of a "Q community" altogether.

The Jesus Seminar also considers the *Gospel of Thomas* to be at least as valuable as the canonical Gospels in determining the shape of the historical Jesus; hence, the *five* Gospels. The dating and value of the *Gospel of Thomas* is a hotbed of debate among scholars. Typically, either one dates it early (60–100 CE) and counts it a (literarily) independent source, or one considers it late (post-140) and dependent upon other Christian literature.

In a nutshell, perusing these sources, the Jesus Seminar scholars determined that, contrary to typical "red-letter" editions, which publish Jesus' words in red font, the historical Jesus is retained only in a fairly small portion of the words (18%) and deeds (16%) recorded in ancient sources. If this were not controversial enough, the "Fellows" also concluded that "Jesus was not born of a virgin, and his father was Joseph or some other male who either seduced or raped Mary. . . . Although Jesus was seen as a healer, he only cured psychosomatic maladies and did not perform any 'nature miracle.'

2. Robert W. Funk and Roy W. Hoover, *The Five Gospels: What Did Jesus Really Say?* Jesus Seminar (Santa Rosa, CA: Polebridge Press, 1994); Robert W. Funk, *Acts of Jesus: What Did Jesus Really Do?* Jesus Seminar (Santa Rosa, CA: Polebridge Press, 1998).

He did not claim to be the Messiah, was executed as a public nuisance, his body decayed, . . . he did not rise bodily from the dead, and there was no empty tomb."[3]

The seminar determined that 12.67% of the sayings from Mark deserved a red/pink vote; on the other hand, 41% of the Q sayings and 22% of the *Thomas* sayings received red/pink. They highlighted the fact that Jesus himself spoke Aramaic; the fact that the Gospels are written at least 20 years later and in Greek obscures his original content. Jesus spoke in pithy aphorisms and parables. He readily used humor and paradox.

Quite contrary to the image presented in the Gospels, Jesus did not actually expect the imminent end of the world. Rather than an apocalyptic prophet shaped by the Hebrew prophets of old, in a heavily apocalyptic form of contemporary Judaism as reflected in texts such as *4 Ezra* (= 2 Esdras) and *1 Enoch*, Jesus was more like a Hellenistic Cynic-sage philosopher. Therefore, the Jesus one finds in Q or *Thomas* more closely approximates the historical Jesus, whereas the Gospel of Mark, upon which much of Matthew and Luke are based, reflects the apocalyptic thinking of the early church.

The Jesus Seminar decided that no saying recorded in the Passion narratives came from the historical Jesus. Mark, the earliest Gospel, reflects the post-Easter Christian community's developing theology *about* Jesus rather than Jesus' own reflection upon his life, ministry, and death. The majority decided that while Jesus certainly considered himself to be anointed with God's Spirit, he did not consider himself *the* Messiah in the later sense of the word.

The historical Jesus was iconoclastic, undermined typical imperial power structures, and declared that God shows special concern for the poor and outcast of society, even when it put him at odds with the religious authorities and doctrines of his own tradition.

That, dear reader, is a lot to contemplate, and you no doubt can see why the seminar has evoked such strong emotion. But before we lose our wits, à la Brown and Johnson, let's consider the positive contributions of the Seminar:

- They, unlike most of us academics, have found a way to engage the larger public in conversation about the historical Jesus.
- They have insisted that the historical Jesus should be freed from church dogma and made available to study using the tools and methods of historical inquiry.
- They have asked us to contemplate seriously whether modern Christians merely retroject onto the historical Jesus their creedal doctrines or economic and political biases.

3. Gowler, *What Are They Saying?* 38.

- They have caused us to ask about proper methodology and sources and whether scholars are driven by theological convictions or critical academic inquiry first and foremost.
- They have sought to work in a collaborative manner and test their results against others.

The deliberations of the Jesus Seminar have evoked swift, strong responses that fall into two main categories: academic considerations and theological considerations.

Academic Considerations

Those who have critiqued the Seminar on academic grounds have raised the following concerns. First, the Jesus Seminar gives the impression that its views are held by the majority of biblical scholars; in fact, their view is simply one among many, and they are a minority voice. That is not to say that they are wrong in their views, but they do not reflect the scholarly consensus that they claim to represent.

Second, the criteria which they have used have been critiqued. They privilege Q and *Thomas* over the Synoptic Gospels. They do not at all consider the Gospel of John to be a reliable historical source. They have not, however, presented a cogent argument as to why John is to be excluded.

Third, they tend to extract Jesus from his Palestinian Jewish context and paint him as a Greek philosopher. It's a short step from Greek philosopher to North American academic. Is their Jesus really a 1st-century Jew who is free to be radically different from the "Fellows," or does he turn out to look surprisingly like the Fellows themselves, who are quite a homogenous group in terms of gender, ethnicity, economic class, education level, and political commitments? It is certainly uncouth to be a Jewish apocalyptic prophet in polite, educated society, but does that mean Jesus was not such?

Theological Considerations

Much of the supposed scholarly debate turns out to be a playground brawl determined by which "team" one belongs to theologically at the outset. The ad hominem attack on display with the historical Jesus is practically unparalleled within the guild of biblical studies. For the most part, the Jesus Seminar and its devotees are reckoned among "liberal Christians" who are reacting to conservative or fundamentalist Christianity, which on the American scene has appeared to dominate considerations of Jesus and Scripture. Those who count themselves on the more conservative side of Christianity feel strongly that the sole quest of the Jesus Seminar is to undermine orthodox, creedal Christianity by painting an almost complete disconnect between the historical Jesus of Nazareth and the risen Christ of Christian faith.

For their part, some of the Fellows react to critique of their scholarship in kind, claiming that those who oppose their views and construct a more "orthodox Jesus" are only manipulating the data for apologetic, doctrinal reasons rather than engaging in objective, disinterested, historical inquiry.

Notable critics of the Jesus Seminar include N. T. Wright, Richard Hays, Ben Witherington III, and Luke Timothy Johnson, all of whom have a clear commitment to "orthodox," even conservative, forms of Christianity. Their own reconstructions of the historical Jesus have been critiques that fall prey to the same dangers that face all Questers: their reconstructed Jesus holds the same convictions they do. The Jesus one needs to find based on one's theological convictions at the outset appears to be the Jesus one arrives at after all of one's arguments have been presented. Funny that.

E. P. Sanders

Working at the same time as the Jesus Seminar, E. P. Sanders has presented quite a different version of the historical Jesus. Sanders's Jesus looks far more Jewish; Jesus is an eschatological prophet with his eye on God's restoration of Israel. While Judaism varied in the 1st century, Sanders argues that covenantal nomism served as a common denominator among all of them. That is, God and Israel enjoyed a covenant; on that basis, Israel was expected to obey God's law, and God was expected to champion Israel and its fate. According to Sanders, Jesus gathered twelve disciples intentionally to indicate the restoration of the twelve tribes of Israel. He proclaimed the kingdom of God and expected an imminent end to Roman rule and the compromised temple, and then the establishment of God's rule with a new restored temple. Jesus, then, was a Jew leading a restoration movement within Judaism; he confined his activity to Israel. Jew though he was, Jesus also found himself in some distinction from his parent tradition because he proclaimed that sinners would be included in God's kingdom even if they did not repent; rather, they needed to accept Jesus, who served a special role in God's kingdom. It may be that Jesus presented himself as a king of sorts, riding into Jerusalem on a donkey, assigning the Twelve a special place in the kingdom. Jesus certainly raised enough suspicions that Rome found it expedient to execute him as a would-be king.

Space does not permit a full presentation of Sanders's Jesus. He has six categories of probability: virtually certain, highly probable, probable, possible, conceivable, and incredible. Let me list only the first and last categories as presented by Gowler:

> Virtually Certain:
> a. Jesus shared the worldview of Jewish restoration eschatology.
> b. He preached the kingdom of God.

c. He promised the kingdom to the wicked.
d. He did not explicitly oppose the law (e.g., Sabbath and food).
e. Neither he nor his disciples thought that the kingdom would be established by the force of arms. They looked for an eschatological miracle.

Incredible:

a. He was one of the rare Jews of his day who believed in love, mercy, grace, repentance, and the forgiveness of sins.
b. Jews in general, and Pharisees in particular, would kill people who believed in such things.
c. Because of his work, Jewish confidence in election was "shaken to pieces," and Judaism as a religion was destroyed.[4]

Sanders has been critiqued on a number of counts, but presently I want to highlight the usefulness of comparing him to the Jesus Seminar. This is not to push the reader to accept one or the other, but to assist you in determining where the fault lines lie in the debate. Unlike some of the work of the Jesus Seminar, (a) Sanders clearly grounds Jesus in Judaism rather than pitting him entirely against the rest of the parent tradition, and (b) he emphasizes the likelihood that Jesus maintained an apocalyptic worldview. In addition, whereas the Jesus Seminar relies so heavily upon Q and the *Gospel of Thomas*, Sanders employs only the Synoptics as a data source. Whereas the Seminar has been critiqued for overreliance on noncanonical materials, Sanders has been critiqued for underemploying them. The Seminar and Sanders do seem to agree, however, on the apparent uselessness of the Gospel of John. More on that later.

For Sanders, Jesus is an eschatological prophet who envisioned the restoration of Israel. In the spirit of the age, he expected God to invade human history definitively and imminently. He saw himself as a key figure in that scenario. Jesus' outlook, however, wasn't just future directed: "Jesus envisioned a new set of power relations in the eschatological kingdom, and this view inherently included social dimensions—a vision of how this new society will function—which has immediate and clear demands for the present."[5]

John Dominic Crossan

If you spend much time watching the History Channel's episodes on Jesus, you will no doubt recognize the face and lilting Irish voice of Crossan. He has devoted much of his life and career to reconstructing the historical Jesus. At this point in his deliberations, Crossan believes that Jesus was an itinerant Jewish peasant who traveled around speaking pithy aphorisms.

4. Ibid., 64–65.
5. Ibid., 72.

Regarding sources used in reconstructing the historical Jesus, Crossan holds the *Gospel of Thomas*, the Egerton Gospel (Papyrus Egerton 2), the *Gospel of the Hebrews*, and the *Gospel of Peter* in high regard, considering them to be independent of the canonical Gospels. Also, Q factors in heavily. This is a minority view among scholars. Again, by *minority*, I do not mean wrong (or right).

In his important work *The Historical Jesus*, Crossan sets out to devise a rigorous methodology for combing through the sources to determine what the historical Jesus would have said, done, and believed. It's a complicated, controversial method that we shall not explore here. As a result of his method, Crossan reconstructs Jesus as an itinerant peasant who preached a radical egalitarianism as opposed to the hierarchical, patron-client system of his day. He sought to build an alternative community where everyone shared material and spiritual resources. He healed, exorcised, and insisted on radical inclusivity at table. He was a Jewish-peasant-Cynic-sage who stood in the wisdom tradition; he was not apocalyptic. Rather, the apocalyptic material was added at a later stage of development of the tradition and imposed upon the image of Jesus. Jesus' eschatology was aimed at nonviolent passive resistance to unjust, evil, oppressive systems.

Because Jesus erased traditional lines of demarcation with respect to gender, class, and purity and denounced current imperial structures imposed by Rome but promulgated by the Herodians, he was bound to come into conflict with authorities. He was eventually killed by Rome, and his body was either devoured by carrion birds or dogs. This, of course, offends some Christians. It would be interesting to discuss this question in a group and ponder why this proposal should or should not be considered problematic by Christians. What's at stake? What do the emotional reactions signify?

Crossan's contributions to the historical Jesus debate are immense, if not all equally useful or compelling. First, he has taught us the importance of attending to the archaeological record when constructing ancient history. Most New Testament scholars rely almost exclusively on texts and ignore the material culture of the period under question. Crossan has reminded us that, politically and economically, 1st-century Palestine was a brutal environment. Numerous people became landless and destitute, with no hope whatsoever of changing their dire circumstances materially. The rich became richer and the poor became poorer. Jesus proclaimed that this situation was radically at odds with God's own vision, and he provided hope for those suffering the worst effects of the unjust system. Whether or not one agrees with Crossan's interpretation of the archaeological evidence, one can no longer countenance the ignoring of such data in any responsible reconstructive project.

It may be that Crossan lends too much weight to the economic and social aspects of Jesus' life and work, but he does serve as a corrective to those who want to downplay the connection between religious, economic, political, and social considerations.[6]

John P. Meier

Another major and prolific player is John P. Meier, whose fourth and final volume of *A Marginal Jew* has only recently been published.[7] According to Meier, Jesus grew up in a Palestine very different from that which Crossan has painted, a much more peaceful, unperturbed environment. He was a follower of John the Baptist, an apocalyptic ascetic who enjoined his fellow Jews to repent in preparation for God's decisive, imminent appearance and judgment. Jesus maintained John's belief that the fruition of God's kingdom was imminent, but his was a more upbeat, less gloomy ministry marked by miraculous healings and exorcisms. Luke 11:20 figures prominently in Meier's construction of Jesus: "If it is by the finger of God that I cast out the demons, then the kingdom of God has come to you." Jesus is an eschatological prophet who performs healings and teaches the followers he has gathered. Like other scholars, Meier decides that Jesus' choice of twelve disciples symbolized his belief that Israel would be restored. According to Meier, Jesus "addressed, challenged, and tried to regather the whole of Israel in the expectation of the imminent end. He was wrong, and he failed."[8]

Meier's reconstruction has been critiqued on various fronts, including methodology, sources, and undue derogation of his colleagues' work.

Gerd Theissen

Like Crossan, Gerd Theissen has devoted many decades to studying the historical Jesus. Using various methodologies, including sociology, psychology, anthropology, and archaeology, Theissen is careful to place Jesus properly into his own social context, noting the ample variety evident in 1st-century varieties of Judaism. Just think about the serious differences among Pharisees, Sadducees, Essenes, and Zealots, to name a few.

Theissen joined forces with Annette Merz to produce *The Historical Jesus: A Comprehensive Guide* (1998) in which they argue that Jesus is best seen as an apocalyptic, itinerant, charismatic, prophetic miracle worker

6. Ibid., 104. For a useful treatment of the economics in that setting, see Morten Hørning Jensen's *Herod Antipas in Galilee* (Tübingen: Mohr Siebeck, 2006).

7. John P. Meier, *A Marginal Jew: Rethinking the Historical Jesus*, vol. 4, *Law and Love* (New Haven, CT: Yale University Press, 2009).

8. Gowler, *What Are They Saying?* 117.

located squarely within Judaism. His ministry was a renewal movement that preached repentance, looked forward to God's restoration of Israel, and viewed Jesus and his disciples as playing a leadership role in that restoration. He traveled from village to village with his message, preaching and healing and pushing against barriers that oppress people. He was lenient regarding purity laws; he welcomed women readily and saw a place for Gentiles in God's plan of salvation. He placed special emphasis on ministry to the poor and marginalized and called for a path of nonviolent resistance against structures that preclude human flourishing. His symbolic actions and words centered on the Jerusalem temple made his enemies seethe, and he was crucified by Rome.

On the spectrum of depictions presented thus far, Theissen and Merz represent a middle ground. Regarding sources, they use both canonical and noncanonical material. Notably, they do not present Jesus as Wisdom (or sage) pitted against Jesus as eschatological prophet. In Jesus they find a figure who represents both (and more!) since both (and more!) were readily available models to him from his Jewish faith.

Marcus Borg

Marcus Borg has captured the attention and imagination of many these days. He speaks far and wide and is avidly read by laypeople. He was one of the early members of the Jesus Seminar and has written a number of books on Jesus. Fortunately, the newcomer to the conversation can get a summary of his views on Jesus in his chapter "Jesus: The Heart of God," in *The Heart of Christianity: Rediscovering a Life of Faith* (2003). He argues that the earlier, traditional view of Jesus—as knowing himself to be Son of God, the Messiah, born of a virgin, dying for our sins, rising physically from the dead, and scheduled to return sooner or later—no longer works for millions of Christians. Using what he calls a "historical-metaphorical approach," Borg, rather than referring to the Jesus of history and the Christ of faith, prefers the categories pre-Easter Jesus and post-Easter Jesus. Since attention to the pre-Easter Jesus, that is, the Jesus who existed in history as a man in Galilee from about 4 BCE to about 30 CE, matters for an incarnational theology, Borg fleshes out some details of the historical figure. He lists six features:

1. Jesus was a Jewish mystic.
2. Jesus was a healer.
3. Jesus was a wisdom teacher.
4. Jesus was a social prophet (like Jeremiah, Isaiah, Amos, and Micah).
5. Jesus was a movement initiator.

6. Jesus was executed for being a social prophet and movement initiator. Jesus was "a radical critic of the domination system who had attracted a following. . . . He was killed because of his politics—because of his passion for God's justice."[9]

Summary

I have provided only the briefest snapshots of the ways some scholars have reconstructed the historical Jesus. But I hope it is enough to show that there are real agreements and disagreements among them, not to mention others whose views have not been presented here. Some common threads that arise include: Jesus as a prophet; Jesus as a miracle worker and healer; Jesus as passionate proclaimer of the kingdom of God; Jesus as concerned with unjust socioeconomic systems; Jesus as a gifted teacher; Jesus as a member of the lower class of his society; Jesus as a resident of Galilee, though becoming itinerant; and Jesus as a Jew, not a Christian (that is, as a man born into, shaped by, and concerned with Judaism, its practices, its Scriptures, its God; remember, there was no such thing as Christianity during the lifetime of the historical Jesus).

Puzzlements

Where Are the Missing Voices?

To date, the vast majority of historical Jesus work published comes from Western, Christian, white males. How would the depiction of Jesus change if more women, non-Westerners, and non-Christians joined the conversation? Paula Fredriksen and Amy-Jill Levine—both Jewish, female, New Testament scholars—have contributed to the discussion. Levine's work *The Misunderstood Jew* is extremely helpful in correcting the problematic notion that Jesus brought everything good that had been missing from Judaism and, in doing so, made it obsolete.[10] Elisabeth Schüssler Fiorenza, whose background is Catholic, depicts Jesus and his followers in terms of a prophetic movement tied to Wisdom-Sophia, which had in view, in part, the liberation of women.[11] More female scholars are wanted in this area. The situation is even direr with respect to non-Western voices.

9. Ibid., 92.
10. Amy-Jill Levine, *The Misunderstood Jew: The Church and the Scandal of the Jewish Jesus* (San Francisco: HarperSanFrancisco, 2006).
11. Elisabeth Schüssler Fiorenza, *Jesus: Miriam's Child, Sophia's Prophet; Critical Issues in Feminist Christology* (New York: Continuum, 1995).

Where Is the Gospel of John?

A severe, intractable problem in historical Jesus research is the largely unquestioned omission of the Gospel of John as a source of data for reconstructing Jesus. This is inexcusable on academic grounds. To remedy this problem, a group of New Testament scholars (including the present author) formed a group at the Society of Biblical Literature in 2002 called "John, Jesus, and History." Its aim is to contest the long-held (but wrong) consensus that John has no claim to historicity and to study how the picture of Jesus would change if John were included. The group has published a number of books to date and continues its work. It has garnered serious attention and is now holding joint sessions with a variety of other groups, including both the Historical Jesus and Synoptic Gospel groups of the Society of Biblical Literature.[12] That promises to be productive for the future of both historical Jesus and Johannine studies.

RECURRING ISSUES

Let's summarize some of the recurring issues that have arisen in our brief presentation.

First, scholars disagree on *which sources* one should use to reconstruct the historical Jesus. We have seen the use of the Synoptic Gospels (but not John), Q, *Gospel of Thomas*, the Egerton Gospel, and the *Gospel of Peter*.

Scholars disagree on *how to date the various sources*. Is *Thomas* early or late? Can one discern strata of chronological development in the Q material? We saw in Crossan's work that if one dates *Thomas* early and finds it independent of the canonical Gospels, and if one considers the Q material early, one will arrive at a nonapocalyptic Jesus.

Once dated, scholars disagree on *how best to use the sources*. Does a word or deed have to appear in more than one independent source to be considered authentic? Should the literary evidence be viewed alone or in concert with archaeological sources?

---

12. See http://johannine.org/JJH.html. So far, the group has published Paul N. Anderson, Felix Just, SJ, and Tom Thatcher, eds., *John, Jesus, and History*, vol. 1, *Critical Appraisals of Critical Views* (Atlanta: Society of Biblical Literature, 2007); and Paul N. Anderson, Felix Just, SJ, and Tom Thatcher, eds., *John, Jesus, and History*, vol. 2, *Aspects of Historicity in the Gospel of John* (Atlanta: Society of Biblical Literature, 2009). The next volume is scheduled to appear in 2011. In addition, the group has published specialized volumes, described at http://catholic-resources .org/SBL/JJH-Books.html.

Second, what kind of Jew was Jesus? Was he apocalyptic or not? Did he see himself as part of the wisdom tradition, the prophetic tradition, both, neither? Did he have a political program in mind (think of the Zealots and Sicarii)? Did he have an ascetic streak (think of John the Baptist and the Essenes)?

Third, what did the sociopolitical terrain of Israel look like? How did life in Galilee differ from life in Jerusalem, if at all? How hellenized was each area, and how do we know? Was Galilee an oasis of peace during Jesus' childhood or a bare-subsistence existence under increasingly unbearable circumstances? Were the urban elites, along with Rome, crushing the life out of rural areas? And was Galilee more urban or rural in the early 1st century? Scholars do not agree on the political and economic scene of 1st-century Galilee.

Fourth, what is the proper relationship between history and theology? Fifth, the epistemological question: How do we properly know and apprehend Jesus?

QUESTIONS, HACKLES, AND WARNINGS RAISED BY THE QUESTS

Like many topics that really matter, the historical Jesus is messy business. Most of us aren't New Testament scholars who spend our days in the minutiae; we are practicing Christians across the theological spectrum, those puzzled by Christianity, those who once were Christian but now have a beef against it, and so on. What does all of this mean for the likes of us in the end? Based on our discussion, here are some points worth pondering:

1. Does the Historical Jesus Really Matter for Christian Faith?

Perhaps yes and no. Yes, the historical Jesus matters insofar as Christians believe in the incarnation—that the Word became flesh and tabernacles among us; that somehow through this unlikely male Jewish artisan in what is now ancient and distant Galilee, God acted decisively for the ultimate salvation of God's world. The Christian God has always gotten involved in the grit, grime, and glory of earthly, finite existence. So it behooves us to learn all we can about this Jesus of Nazareth historically. Furthermore, it is *this* Jesus of Nazareth whom Christians proclaim was raised from the dead by God and lives and acts in the world to this day.

On the other hand—No, the historical Jesus doesn't matter all that much. That is to say, Christian theology has proceeded for many centuries without interest in or reference to the historical Jesus debates. Today is no different.

Historical Jesus research has produced myriad Jesuses, from Funk's secular, iconoclastic hippie to N. T. Wright's orthodox Anglican. New Testament scholars can barely keep up with all these Jesuses, so how can we expect those of another field to navigate these stormy seas? It tends to be the Jesus of the creeds who reigns supreme among ordinary Christians in the pews. This is true even for "noncreedal," "free-church" Christians.

2. "Buddy Jesus": The Domestication of the Savior of the World

While not able to provide a definitive picture of the historical Jesus, these scholars have certainly raised enough issues to make us all take stock of whether we have created Jesus in our own image. Most Christians, not just historical Jesus scholars, are guilty of domesticating Jesus, making him palatable or at least "relevant" to our own traditions and life circumstances at any given moment. If you are a "liberal" Christian, you will gravitate toward the Jesus of Marcus Borg or John Dominic Crossan. If you are "orthodox" or "conservative," you will adore the Jesus of N. T. Wright (Anglican conservative) or Ben Witherington III (evangelical). If you are a poor, marginalized Christian, you will worship Jesus the eschatological prophet who damns the rich and proclaims the imminent inbreaking of God, who will exalt the lowly and humble the proud. If you are an educated, urbane Christian, you will shy away from the odd apocalyptic prophet and affirm the Jesus who is interested in creating just systems here and now, so that egalitarianism and democracy of some sort may reign. And so on.

Your personal life stage will also affect your view of Jesus. As the renowned New Testament scholar Dale Allison confesses in his wonderfully helpful recent book *The Historical Christ and the Theological Jesus* (2009), he wrote one of his historical Jesus books during a particularly depressing, rather hopeless period in his own life. The Jesus he came up with at that time was the Jesus he needed. If he were to write the book today, Jesus would come out differently.

So the reader is encouraged to take stock in an honest way of his or her political leanings and current life circumstances and how those affect one's view of Jesus.

3. Resist the Tabloids: Choose the Narrow Gate and/or Ask Scholars to Widen It

You, reader, are an extremely busy person. I know this. But you are also an engaged person, interested in deepening your knowledge and faith. You often grocery shop. At the checkout, you are bombarded with whatever latest "discovery" has occurred related to the Bible—the James ossuary, the Jesus ossuary, the recently discovered gospel that changes the entire landscape of Christianity. Notice that these "discoveries" and "important controversies" appear especially around Christmas and Easter, two times of the year when the media and their money-making machines have a captive audience in the form of you. Be *very* skeptical of these sensational tactics. If you have to choose between gripping, entertaining, but intellectually dubious offerings and the dry, somewhat mind-numbing deliberations, choose the latter. Better yet, insist that we Christian academics do a better job of sharing our thoughts in an entertaining, accessible manner! Just because a scholar is popular with the media does not mean he or she is correct or represents the majority view of scholars. In fact, the minute someone makes such a claim, become skeptical.

4. Does W(hat) W(ould) J(esus) D(o) matter?

Once we have made space for a historical Jesus who may, in fact, be very different from us and not always share our same concerns or viewpoints, let us ask this question, put so well by Gowler: "For those who are interested, the challenge remains: How to modernize Jesus authentically without anachronizing or domesticating him."[13] As Christians, we are interested in what happened "back in the day" with Jesus and his people. But quite pressing is the question "So what?" What does it have to do with you and me and how we live our lives as individuals and communities? What if we find ourselves in disagreement with the historical Jesus? What if he did not speak to issues that keep you and me awake at night? Do we abandon those concerns of ours or do we ask, "What Would Jesus Do?" in our situation?

5. Continuity/Discontinuity

Is there continuity between the Jesus of history and Christ of faith, or did early Christians just fabricate him to serve their own ends? How much did the historical Jesus have in common with the early church? How much does he have in common with the myriad versions of the contemporary church?

6. Jesus' Self-Understanding

How does the analysis of the historical Jesus impact ideas about the divinity of Christ? Are we really to believe that Jesus of Nazareth spoke and understood

13. Gowler, *What Are They Saying?* 140.

all of the world's languages of his day? What titles, if any, did the historical Jesus use for himself? He spoke of the Son of Man, no doubt. Did he imagine himself to be that figure while he was living? Did he imagine himself to be God in his own lifetime? If he didn't consider himself God or the Son of Man, what does that mean for the cross? Was he a social revolutionary who met an unjust end, with his hopes and dreams nailed to the cross along with his hands and feet, surprised that God did not rescue him at the last minute? Or was he a more Socratic or Martin Luther King Jr. figure who understood that his actions would most likely lead to death but that truth and integrity demanded that he stay the path no matter what?

7. Capacious Dialogue

Understand that deep disagreement exists among scholars who are equally faithful and intelligent. Try to listen to all sides and allow it to stretch your own thinking and faith, however uncomfortable.

8. History and Theology

What impact do these questions and answers have on theology? For instance, history cannot adjudicate certain matters. The creeds claim that Jesus was born of a virgin. History points to Jesus being the son of Mary and Joseph and having at least four brothers and sisters. Are these mutually exclusive items? If he wasn't born of a virgin, what does this mean for salvation? What does it mean for Mary's role in Christian tradition and piety? If the historical Jesus did not apprehend himself as the Messiah, the Son of Man, Lady Wisdom, Lord, and/or God, what does that mean for the Christian doctrine of the Trinity?

For an engaging, honest read about the way theology and historical Jesus studies can and can't inform one another, read Dale Allison's *The Historical Christ and the Theological Jesus* (notice the play on words: usually it's put as the Historical Jesus and the Theological Christ). He speaks as a Christian and scholar who has devoted his career to historical Jesus studies. He believes that Christians should *absolutely* be curious about and interested in historical Jesus studies. But he also knows that, finally, it is the Jesus of the Gospels who has inspired, sustained, and transformed millions of people over the centuries.

As a historical Jesus scholar, he is skeptical about our ability to determine whether a particular story, word, or deed of Jesus can be certainly traced back to the Nazarene. But he stands convinced that the Gospels indubitably show us the Jesus who matters most deeply. How? "We need to quit pretending to do what we cannot do. The Gospels are parables. When we read them, we should think not that Jesus said this or did that but rather: Jesus did things like this, and he said things like that."[14]

I must, however, take Allison to task for his inexplicable and inexcusable exclusion of the Jesus material from the Gospel of John. Using his own reasoning, it should be imperative to include all of the material found in the Gospel of John. Reader, take advantage of Allison's valuable insights, but avoid his egregious error; go even deeper than he does by allowing the Gospel of John to inform you as much as the Synoptics do.

Allison insists that we must ask about the historical Jesus and learn all we can to be faithful. He also acknowledges the limitations of the tools. Furthermore, he highlights an important fact that I hope the reader finds as a theme throughout the current book: all interpreters bring certain tools and presuppositions and agendas to the biblical text and these, to some extent, determine what the interpreter finds in the texts. Check out his example regarding the Little Apocalypse in Mark 13 (if you have no idea what I'm talking about here, stop and read Mark 13). Addressing Mark 13:26, which tells us that the Son of Man will come on the clouds of heaven, Allison imagines four different readers:

> a fundamentalist, a liberal Protestant, a sympathetic non-Christian, and an unsympathetic non-Christian. All four, let us say, agree that the Evangelist Mark expected someday to look up into the sky and to see Jesus riding the clouds. After that, agreement fails. The fundamentalist claims that Mark's literal understanding is binding for interpretation; we, too, should look to the skies, from whence Jesus our Savior will someday return. Our liberal Protestant responds that, whatever the ancients thought, people cannot ride on clouds, so we are compelled to view Mark 13:26 as a mythological statement: the verse is a way of affirming that the God of Jesus Christ will set things right in the end. The sympathetic non-Christian, disbelieving in a deity, disagrees with both the fundamentalist and the liberal and instead finds the real meaning of Mark 13:26 to lie in the fact that people always need hope, even if it is only hope in a myth. The unsympathetic non-Christian then retorts that Jesus has not returned and will never return, and so the true meaning of Mark 13:26 is that Christians are deluded, their faith vain.

The lesson to draw from our four exegetes is that a text is never the sole determinant of its interpretation or application. Readings are rather joint productions; they require not only judgment as to what a text meant to those in the

---

14. Allison, *The Historical Christ*, 66.

past but also judgment as to what it should or can mean in the present, and the latter involves convictions extrinsic to the texts themselves.[15]

Allison insists, however, that studying the historical Jesus can deeply impact and maybe even change one's views on Christian faith; that has been his experience, to be sure. Will it be yours? How has it mattered for him, and how might it therefore matter for us?

Christology

Studying the historical Jesus has affected Allison's Christology, his view of the life and work of Christ. In short, conservatives may have too high a Christology and liberals too low. The truth may be somewhere in between for Allison. Conservatives imagine that Jesus took himself to be God, the second person of the Trinity. In so doing, they tend to downplay the distinctions that Jesus maintained between himself and God as well as the reality and depth of his suffering. The Gospels depict him as truly getting angry, tired, hesitant, and as not omniscient. Orthodox theology tries to explain these passages away.

Remember the movie *Dogma* with "Buddy Christ"? This is the sin of the liberals: they picture Jesus as merely human, or in the words of Joan Osborne, "just a slob like one of us." But according to Allison, the historical Jesus did envision himself as playing a unique role in God's unfolding plan for our salvation, different from the roles you and I adopt. Historical Jesus studies can discomfit both sides and move both closer to truth.

Eschatology

Jesus most likely expected the end of the world in his own lifetime or soon afterward. That has not happened. Many Christians cannot countenance a Jesus who erred on this count so they conduct all kinds of exegetical acrobatics to rescue Jesus from his errors. But Allison invites us moderns to leave behind the literal and understand that eschatology is powerful in figurative terms; it's the basis of hope. This does not mean that the historical Jesus operated in figurative terms; he likely believed in a literal, imminent end. But already in the New Testament texts, such as the Gospel of John, we see a move to the mythical or the figurative in terms of eschatology. The New Testament, not to mention Jesus himself, is full of both/and; it does not appear to insist heavily on either/or, as many of us do.

In the end, Allison teaches us that studying the historical Jesus imbues us simultaneously with both healthy theological confidence and healthy theological humility.

15. Ibid., 38–39.

STUDY QUESTIONS

1. Do you and your church sympathize most with Allison's fundamentalist, liberal Protestant, sympathetic non-Christian, or unsympathetic non-Christian?
2. Have you ever heard of the historical Jesus debate before now? If you have heard of it before, what have you learned in this discussion that challenged or clarified that prior understanding?
3. Does the historical Jesus matter to you? Why or why not?
4. In your own theology and that of your church, what percent human and what percent divine is Jesus? When Jesus says, "My God, my God, why have you forsaken me?" (Matt. 27:46; Mark 15:34), what do you and your church make of it? How about when he says, "But about that day or hour no one knows, neither the angels of heaven, nor the Son, but only the Father" (Mark 13:32)? If he's God, how can he not know? Does he actually know but is telling some kind of "white lie" here?

7

The Politics of Biblical Interpretation

The Bible is an open book. Women and men from a variety of theological traditions, ethnic communities, economic strata, ages, physical conditions, and sexual orientations have been reading it for centuries. At different times, people in all of these circumstances have found themselves empowered by the Bible, challenged by it, confused by it, restricted by it, and harmed by it. They have sought to understand it, to interpret it, to control it, to obey it, and to escape it. People love the Bible as a source of life and light and truth and hope. And sometimes they hate its power.

Frederick C. Tiffany and Sharon Ringe[1]

You and I are somewhat similar, somewhat different, and that matters greatly for how we interpret the Bible. Our age, gender, race, ethnicity, social class, religious affiliations (or lack thereof), childhood experiences, personality types (think Enneagram and Myers-Briggs), life experiences, where we're from, where we're going or would like to go—all of these are part and parcel of what makes us us and influence how we interact with the Bible. Perhaps this kind of statement strikes you as absurd or as "political correctness run amok." Bear with me. Set aside your defenses for the moment and enter the "thought experiment" that is this chapter. You are not agreeing or disagreeing with me, and you are certainly not committing to anything. If the exercise turns out to be useless, you can chuck it and move on. Deal?

Biblical studies has learned much from feminist, womanist, *mujerista*, liberationist, disability, and postcolonial analysis, and from sex and gender studies

---

1. Frederick C. Tiffany and Sharon Ringe, *Biblical Interpretation: A Roadmap* (Nashville: Abingdon Press, 1996), 13.

more generally, but the fruits of those interdisciplinary engagements have not yet been fully realized in church preaching and teaching. This chapter will present contemporary scholarly thinking on gender, race, class, and culture issues in New Testament studies, with particular attention to constructions of identity and boundaries. In addition, we will ask about the dynamic between author, text, and reader in determining interpretive meaning.

Until fairly recently, published, authoritative biblical interpretation was conducted only by men, particularly white men. Lately, other voices have joined the conversation, though sometimes unbidden and unwelcome. I myself attended Yale for both seminary (1990–93) and doctoral work (1993–2000). Note that as a seminarian I had one (white) female Bible professor; the rest were all white males. As a doctoral student, every single professor I had from 1993 to 2000 was an older white male (all wonderful people, to whom I am deeply indebted to this day. My comment is not personal—it's sociological). Imagine yourself in my position as a white female professor introducing students to the critical study of the Bible in Dallas, Texas, in 2010. What should I use as a basic textbook, if anything?

In fall 2009, I made a pedagogical mistake. I used Luke Timothy Johnson's *The Writings of the New Testament: An Interpretation* as the "main" textbook and "supplemented" it with several other resources, including *True to Our Native Land: An African American New Testament Commentary*, *The Women's Bible Commentary*, and the *Theological Bible Commentary*. Now, there's nothing wrong per se with Johnson's textbook—indeed, I myself learned from it 20 years ago in my seminary intro course. The problem lay in the impression rendered that Johnson's white, male, Episcopalian, Yale-trained, historical-critical-with-a-touch-of-theology-and-literary-sensitivities approach was the "objective, unbiased truth of the matter," whereas the other resources represented "ideological, special-interest political approaches to the text." Furthermore, it was noted early on that I had not included any resources that represented the GLBTQ (gay, lesbian, bisexual, transgendered, queer/questioning) voices. I quickly sent out GLBTQ sources, but the tone had already been set by the syllabus.

I remedied this situation in Spring 2010 by eliminating any notion of a primary textbook whereby one voice reigned authoritative. Instead, I rotated the various resources as the main textbook on any given day. One day we discussed the African American commentary as the primary textbook; another day it was the *Theological Bible Commentary*. Another day the *Women's Bible Commentary*. Each resource has a very specific focus. What's fabulous is that some of the same scholars appear in the different resources, though donning different methodological and interpretive concerns. So Brad Braxton, Michael Brown, and Allen Dwight Callahan write for both *True to Our Native*

Land as well as the *Theological Bible Commentary*. In each instance, the agenda and approach of the method dictate what they comment upon and the rhetoric employed. When Michael Brown writes on Romans for the *Theological Bible Commentary*, we hear much about sin and justification without much reference to particular African American social location. When he writes on Matthew in *True to Our Native Land: An African-American Commentary on the New Testament*, however, Brown adduces references to Nelson Mandela, focuses upon the Africanism of the church father Tertullian, draws upon the womanist scholar Renita Weems, quotes the poet Maya Angelou (re Matt. 7:1–29), Martin Luther King Jr. and Sojourner Truth (re Matt. 8:1–9:38), Frederick Douglass (re Matt 9:1–8), and so on.

Gail O'Day contributes to (and indeed coedits) the *Theological Bible Commentary*; she also contributes to the *Women's Bible Commentary*. The same is true of E. Elizabeth Johnson, Patricia Tull, and Joanna Dewey. In each case, they focus on the particular agenda of the resource. The *Women's Bible Commentary* is

> the first comprehensive attempt to gather some of the fruits of feminist biblical scholarship on each book of the Bible in order to share it with the larger community of women who read the Bible. . . . Rather than asking the contributors to comment on each and every section of the biblical book, we have followed the model of Elizabeth Cady Stanton's *Woman's Bible* and asked contributors to select for comment those passages that they have judged to be of particular relevance to women. What contributors have selected includes not only portions of the Bible that deal explicitly with female characters and symbols but also sections that bear on the condition of women more generally. Aspects of social life, marriage and family, the legal status of women, religious and economic institutions, the ways in which community boundaries were defined and maintained, and other such topics are all treated.[2]

In the *Theological Bible Commentary*,

> theological reflection is not centered on favorite or seminal passages, nor on scholarly constructions of the biblical material and its theological trajectories (e.g., the Deuteronomistic History, the Tetrateuch, Q, the historical Jesus), nor on overarching theological themes— "covenant," justification by faith," "creation," "incarnation"—whose roots are in the biblical material. This biblical theological commentary is *textual* theological reflection, contingent on the fully formed biblical books. Further, this approach does not privilege one biblical

---

2. Carol A. Newsom and Sharon H. Ringe, eds., *The Women's Bible Commentary* (Louisville, KY: Westminster John Knox Press, 1998), xxi–xxiv.

book over another. This volume is not predicated upon the notion of a theological center or fulcrum for either the Old or New Testament. Each biblical book serves as the basis for theological reflection in this commentary. . . . As a whole, the volume invites the reader to engage the biblical books themselves and their exegetical details as the stuff of theological reflection.[3]

Far from implying that these scholars who write for multiple methodological commentaries are conflicted regarding "the" meaning of a given biblical book or passage, each demonstrates that we come to the Bible with different foci, questions, and methods on different days for different purposes. All are important, valid, and potentially life giving. Each of us must learn to be honest about what we are looking for with each approach to the texts; for surely what we seek in large part determines what we find and what we leave for future discovery for some other day, for some other set of questions or line of inquiry.

I do not want to give my students (or you the reader) the impression that there is any "objective, unbiased" interpretation to be had from our Scriptures. The scholar operating from the historical-critical approach is just as biased and politically-theologically motivated as the one operating from a feminist perspective. In a way, I hate that the *Women's Bible Commentary* is named thus, since it tends to imply that the material therein pertains just to women, rather than to all people. Surely issues highlighting women and pertinent to women in history are germane to all human beings. The same problem arises when one tries to teach a series on "women in the Bible" or "feminist approaches to Scripture." Often, only women show up. But surely any issues regarding gender are pertinent to all people, not just women. Likewise, when one teaches a course on "African American Interpretation of the Bible," it is arguably unfortunate that such a course is populated primarily by African Americans. Are these not broader concerns that affect us all?

FEMINIST BIBLICAL INTERPRETATION: A TALE OF TWO ELIZ(S)ABETHS

One could date the rise of feminist biblical criticism to the 19th century, with Elizabeth Cady Stanton and the *Woman's Bible*. But most would credit Elisabeth Schüssler Fiorenza with producing the flood of scholarship that has never been stemmed since the appearance of her book *In Memory of Her:*

---

3. Gail R. O'Day and David L. Petersen, eds., *Theological Bible Commentary* (Louisville, KY: Westminster John Knox Press, 2009), vii–viii.

A Feminist Theological Reconstruction of Christian Origins (1983). Feminist interpreters maintain that the Bible has been systematically used to oppress women religiously, socially, and economically. The Bible was written by men for men, and men have perpetuated interpretations that promote an "androcentric (i.e., male-centered), patriarchal (i.e., male-dominative), and sexist (i.e., discriminatory toward and oppressive of women)" ethos.[4] The spectrum of feminist approaches is wide—some feminists find the biblical text irredeemable as an authoritative text that reveals God and creates space for an encounter with the risen Christ; others devote their scholarly careers to helping us find that which is salvific, liberating for women and, indeed, for all of creation.

Feminists employ many different strategies to retrieve or recover the presence of women in the Bible.[5]

Let's start with translation issues. Often the way translators translate a text renders women invisible. For instance, the Greek word *adelphoi* is the plural form of the word "brother." In Greek, if one is speaking to a group that includes both men and women, Greek uses the masculine plural (grammatically speaking, the masculine is the "unmarked" category). Thus, when Paul addresses his Roman audience in 10:1 with *adelphoi*, he is speaking to both men and women. It would therefore be inaccurate to translate the word literally as "brothers." Hence the NRSV translates it as "brothers and sisters" though technically there is only one word there to be translated.

Romans 16 exemplifies an even more pernicious type of translation problem. In verse 1 Phoebe is called a *diakonos* of the church in Cenchreae. This word is variously rendered in English as "servant" (CSB, KJV, NAS), "deaconess" (New Jerusalem Bible), "deacon" (NRSV), and "minister" (NAB). When Paul uses this word of Phoebe, he does not feminize it, so we can rule out the translation "deaconess" altogether. In fact, *diakonos* is exactly the same word Paul uses in 1 Corinthians 3:5 to speak of himself and Apollos—surely they are not "deaconesses"! This translation displays a political move to belittle Phoebe's role or office. She is a minister, like Paul and Apollos.

Later in the chapter Paul refers to Junia and calls her a prominent *apostolos*, which, as you've guessed, means apostle. You may or may not be surprised to learn that later scribes added an "s" to Junia to make her name Junias thereby making her a man with one pen stroke. Again, some people cannot bear the thought of a female apostle and will do whatever they deem necessary to erase the record of such women through sly, subtle moves that are lost on

4. Sandra M. Schneiders, *Written That You May Believe: Encountering Jesus in the Fourth Gospel* (New York: Herder & Herder, 2003), 127.

5. I suggest that you read Sarah Heaner Lancaster, *Women and the Authority of Scripture: A Narrative Approach* (Harrisburg, PA: Trinity Press International, 2002).

most Christian readers. And we could list numerous other examples of this demoting type of move made by translators whose agenda includes excluding women from church leadership.

Another strategy involves highlighting positive texts about women. Here we could name the Samaritan woman of John 4, who engages Jesus in deep theological dialogue and then proceeds to testify about him to her neighbors such that they believe and are saved. Or we could discuss the women who are the first to receive resurrection appearances of Jesus. This is a helpful technique, but one that must be used with caution. To extract stories from the Bible "about women" implies that the rest of the stories are *not* about women, that women appear only in exceptional cases, that the overarching story is really about God and men, with women as minor characters at best.

Feminist critics also challenge assumptions that readers bring to the texts. For example, none of the canonical Gospels name their author; yet most people assume that each was written by a male. In fact, people seem to assume that each Gospel was written by only one hand. It may be that both assumptions are wrong. Indeed, it has been suggested that both Luke and John were written wholly or in part by a woman.

Correcting misinterpretations of texts constitutes part of feminist work. In an earlier chapter, we observed the tendency for interpreters to identify Mary Magdalene as a prostitute. The biblical text never once intimates such an identity; thus not only does Magdalene not get her due, which the Bible gives her as a prominent witness and proclaimer, but she also gets vilified. The same happens to the Samaritan woman, who is often called a whore, if she is preached about at all. Yet the text says she had husbands, not customers.

All feminists would argue that biblical interpretation carries ethical responsibility. To interpret texts in a way that places power into the hands of a particular group and denies power to others is unethical. It's not surprising, then, that another set of voices arose in the form of black feminist interpreters in America who argued that feminist biblical criticism was racist insofar as it was conducted by white women operating solely from the experience of white women, using white sources and then universalizing that experience as if it represented all women. Thus was born "womanist" biblical criticism and theology, a term taken from Alice Walker. In her influential work *White Women's Christ and Black Women's Jesus: Feminist Christology and Womanist Response*, Jacquelyn Grant exposes the ways feminist theology was insufficient, bourgeois and, most importantly, did not recognize the triple dimension of the oppression suffered by black women due to the collusion of race, gender, and class.

Mujerista theology adds yet another set of voices to the ways gender, race, and ethnicity intersect with biblical interpretation. This is theology done from an expressly Hispanic feminist perspective. To be sure, in the United

States alone one can see that the experience of Hispanic women differs greatly from both white women and black women. How much more so when one moves to the global context.

QUEER COMMENTARY

Attention to gender issues as part of biblical interpretation has expanded to include vital voices from the lesbian, gay, bisexual, and transgendered communities as well. There is a growing conversation about the ways gender is constructed by cultures and societies and how that impinges upon the act of reading the Bible. A group knows it has "arrived" in the guild of biblical studies to some degree when there is a commentary tied to the method and it is released by a well-regarded publishing house. Such is the case with *The Queer Bible Commentary* which

> demonstrates . . . that these texts will not be bound but, rather, have the ever-surprising capacity to be disruptive, unsettling and unexpectedly but delightfully queer. Moreover, this commentary provides ample demonstration that this queerness can be found, not just in a handful of selected texts, but across the board in every text of the First and Second Testaments. Contributors take seriously both how reading from lesbian, gay, bisexual and/or transgender perspectives affects[s] the reading and interpretation of biblical texts and how biblical texts have and do affect lesbian, gay, bisexual and/or transgender communities. Politically and religiously engaged, disruptive of both sex-gender-sexuality norms and academic conventions, playful and at times purposefully irreverent, here academic and lay readers will find a commentary unlike all other commentaries. . . . Contributors to this volume focus specifically upon . . . issues such as the construction of gender and sexuality, the reification of heterosexuality, the complicated question of lesbian and gay ancestry within the Bible, the transgendered voices of the prophets, the use of the Bible in contemporary political, socio-economic and religious spheres and the impact of its contemporary interpretation upon lesbian, gay, bisexual and transgender communities.[6]

RACE AND ETHNICITY

As with all of the above, whole books and commentaries can be and are written about the ways that race and ethnicity intersect with biblical interpretation. I have already mentioned the African American commentary that I use

6. Deryn Guest, Robert E. Goss, Mona West, and Thomas Bohache, eds., *The Queer Bible Commentary* (London: SCM Press, 2006), xiii.

in my course, but please realize that there are many others available as well, including Asian American, Hispanic American, and Native American.

Moving beyond the American context to the global scene, one is treated to a veritable cornucopia of perspectives.

POSTCOLONIALISM

Drawing upon Jacques Lacan, Jacques Derrida, and Michel Foucault, postcolonial biblical interpretation, a more recent approach, critiques the imperialist assumptions evident in much of the history of biblical interpretation as well as within the Bible itself. Attention to the global economy and especially the status of the two-thirds world must be part of responsible biblical interpretation. The Bible contains numerous stories about Israel driving native peoples out of their lands, decimation, genocide, massive violence—all supposedly in accordance with God's will. Certainly Christians have used and continue to use such conquest stories to justify conquering and colonizing various populations. Empires are ravenous creatures whose gluttonous drive to consume destroys human beings and creation; where the biblical texts are used to promote destruction rather than the flourishing of all creation, sin reigns. As my colleague Theo Walker is wont to say, based on Luke 4:18, "If it's not good news for the poor, it's not good news." Postcolonial criticism recognizes that race, gender, ethnicity, and economics all work together to oppress the many and privilege the few. Until recently, most biblical scholarship has been conducted by white, Western, moneyed males. No longer. To see the growing variety of voices from around the world producing biblical scholarship, take a look at the *Global Bible Commentary* (2004). To see the important, impressive fruits of postcolonial scholarship, check out the new *Postcolonial Commentary on the New Testament Writings* (2009). As S. Moore notes:

> postcolonial studies is by no means narrowly focused on the twin phenomena of colonialism and postcolonialism. A series of other, related phenomena also fall within its orbit: imperialism, Orientalism, universalism, expansionism, exploration, invasion, enslavement, settlement, resistance, revolt, terrorism, nationalism, nativism, negritude, assimilation, creolization, hybridization, colonial mimicry, the subaltern, marginalization, migration, diasporization, decolonization, globalization, and neocolonialism—all intersected by the ubiquitous determinants of language, gender, race, ethnicity, and class. The relevance of many of these concepts to the biblical texts, considered even in their ancient milieu, hardly needs belaboring.[7]

7. Stephen D. Moore, "Postcolonialism," in *Handbook of Postmodern Biblical Interpretation*, ed. A. K. M. Adam (St. Louis: Chalice Press, 2000), 185–86.

DISABILITY THEORY AND BIBLICAL INTERPRETATION

One of the newest forms of biblical criticism is that stemming from disability theory, which seeks to address the oppression of those labeled as disabled. The Bible has certainly contributed to the marginalization of those with physical disabilities. From the purity codes of Leviticus, which disdain that which is "blemished," to passages and sermons that refer to various characters by their disease alone (the demoniac, the epileptic, the blind, the lame, the deaf), persons with disabilities have been viewed as "lesser than" other persons. Like the other ideological critics discussed thus far, these scholars attend to the economic, political, social, cultural, and religious aspects of the ways disability is defined, experienced, and managed by groups and individuals. Who has the power to define and label what constitutes a disability? We have an abundance of such questions surrounding us in our current context. For insurance purposes, for example, perfectly healthy pregnancies are often considered under the category of "disability"! What does it mean when the huge, wealthy church right next to my seminary has a choir loft that is inaccessible to those in wheelchairs? A person whose spiritual gift is singing cannot serve in the church choir? Huh? And what of the fact that only in 2009 did my seminary become handicapped-accessible? How does this cohere with the biblical witness? On the one hand, it propagates the problematic attitudes in Scripture and eclipses the liberative potential located in the same canon that focuses upon the interdependence of every single member of Christ's body. Recall what Paul says in 1 Corinthians 12:19–27:

> If all were a single member, where would the body be? As it is, there are many members, yet one body. The eye cannot say to the hand, "I have no need of you," nor again the head to the feet, "I have no need of you." On the contrary, the members of the body that seem to be weaker are indispensable, and those members of the body that we think less honorable we clothe with greater honor, and our less respectable members are treated with greater respect; whereas our more respectable members do not need this. But God has so arranged the body, giving the greater honor to the inferior member, that there may be no dissension within the body, but the members may have the same care for one another. If one member suffers, all suffer together with it; if one member is honored, all rejoice together with it. Now you are the body of Christ and individually members of it.

Wasn't it the apostle Paul himself who reveled in the irony of the language of weak and strong as used by the world versus the way God sees things?

> For God's foolishness is wiser than human wisdom, and God's weakness is stronger than human strength.

Consider your own call, brothers and sisters: not many of you were wise by human standards, not many were powerful, not many were of noble birth. But God chose what is foolish in the world to shame the wise; God chose what is weak in the world to shame the strong; God chose what is low and despised in the world, things that are not, to reduce to nothing things that are, so that no one might boast in the presence of God. (1 Cor. 1:25–29)

But if I wish to boast, I will not be a fool, for I will be speaking the truth. But I refrain from it, so that no one may think better of me than what is seen in me or heard from me, even considering the exceptional character of the revelations. Therefore, to keep me from being too elated, a thorn was given me in the flesh, a messenger of Satan to torment me, to keep me from being too elated. Three times I appealed to the Lord about this, that it would leave me, but he said to me, "My grace is sufficient for you, for power is made perfect in weakness." So, I will boast all the more gladly of my weaknesses, so that the power of Christ may dwell in me. Therefore I am content with weaknesses, insults, hardships, persecutions, and calamities for the sake of Christ; for whenever I am weak, then I am strong. (2 Cor. 12:6–10)

Kathy Black notes that much interpretation denies agency to persons with disabilities: "We tend to use them [the people in the biblical stories who are disabled or 'differently-abled'] as objects to make some other point. The problem with this is that persons with disabilities today likewise find themselves treated as objects. Health care, education, employment, social services—all the basic institutions of our society often view persons with disabilities as objects to be dealt with, rather than as subjects that have something to contribute."[8]

In his tentatively titled book *The Bible, Disability, and the Church: A New Vision of the People of God* (Eerdmans, forthcoming), Amos Yong argues that:

In fact, the whole church cannot be the whole (healed) people of God apart from people with disabilities! Hence the church is not only hospitable to and inclusive of people with disabilities, but also receives the hospitality and gifts of people with disabilities for the building up of the wider body. In this way, the church shifts from being a congregation of able-bodied people who welcome people with disabilities, to being a people of differing abilities through whom the many gifts of the Holy Spirit are distributed for the edification of the church in its ministries. In the end, then, there is no "we" who include "them" but an "us" who are mutually defined by the various gifts of the Spirit that empowers every member of the body of Christ to bear the love of God to the world. (personal correspondence, March 12, 2010)

8. Kathy Black, *A Healing Homiletic: Preaching and Disability* (Nashville: Abingdon Press, 1996), 13.

At present, there is no full-scale commentary devoted to biblical interpretation from a disability theory approach, though I suspect that lacuna to be quickly filled.

SUMMARY

People tend to categorize these approaches as "ideological criticism." Is it accurate to lump all of these methods under the same umbrella? What do they have in common, if anything? On a positive note, some may say that they are conjoined by a commitment to political liberation of particular groups. For some the word "ideological" has a negative connotation—those whose approach is "ideological" allow their own values and biases to influence their scholarship. Ideological critics would not repudiate that claim; rather, they would argue that there is no such thing as value-free research and results since we are all (traditional or innovative, modernist or postmodernist, conservative or liberal) bound to particular ideologies whether we are aware of them and honest about them or not.

AN EXERCISE IN IDEOLOGY CRITICISM

Think of a church in your nearest city that would be considered "very successful" by the categories of modern American society. Describe the senior pastor. When I did this exercise with my students, no holds barred, the pastor emerged as a white, documented, heterosexual, married male in his forties or fifties with children, white teeth, physically healthy, not bald, educated, well-dressed, covered by health insurance, with a substantial income.

What if Galatians 3:28 were taken as a motto for the church: "There is no longer Jew or Greek, there is no longer slave or free, there is no longer male and female; for all of you are one in Christ Jesus"? That is, what if Christians did not buy into the supremacy of binary, hierarchical categories so beloved by those who lust for power? With the Jew/Greek, Paul adduces national, racial, and ethnic categories; slave/free relates to economic and legal status; male/female to gender constructs. When I ask my students to name analogous modern categories, they say male/female, gay/straight, old/young, documented/undocumented, black/white, black/Hispanic, healthy/ill, rich/poor, educated/uneducated, citizen/noncitizen. If we were to imagine a Christian pastor who represented the "negative" element of each of the above categories, what would she look like? Maybe something like the old black woman from Alice Walker's story "The Welcome Table," who shows up at the "wrong" (i.e., white) church one Sunday and is duly dispensed with? Maybe the pastor would be an old, illiterate, female, black, lesbian, poor, wheelchair-bound person. Would anyone follow her lead? Would such a church become wildly successful? Why or why not? What does this say about power dynamics in our culture and which people are more or less valued?

THE RESIDENCE OF MEANING(S): AUTHORS, TEXTS, READERS

Authors?

The act of biblical interpretation involves readers, texts, and authors, but how does each relate to the determination of textual meaning? Traditional modernist interpretation assumes that an author (singlehandedly) wrote a text in antiquity, and the modern reader (reading alone silently to himself or herself) is to discern what the ancient author's original intent was when he (the author is usually assumed to be male) composed the text for the original ancient audience. Thus the meaning lies within the author's intent as conveyed through the text and should be extracted from that text by the reader who acts as an archaeologist or historian.

In 1946 Wimsatt and Beardslee, literary scholars of the New Criticism method, published a provocative essay called "The Intentional Fallacy," in which they argued that the intent of the original author is not important to determining the meaning of a text. That is, the meaning must be sought in the text, not in the author's intent. For instance, the apostle Paul is dead so we can't ask him what his intent was. Even if we could, it wouldn't help us much since (a) he may have intended one thing but failed to achieve his intent, or (b) he may have produced something besides or in addition to what he thought he intended.

Texts?

According to the New Critics, the only appropriate material for the literary critic is the internal material of the piece of literature itself: the syntax, the structure, the form. In a way, one might say that the author does not speak; the text speaks. But this assumption has also been questioned. For example, Dale Martin titles the first chapter in his *Sex and the Single Savior: Gender and Sexuality in Biblical Interpretation* (2006) as "The Myth of Textual Agency." In it he squarely warns against being lulled into any notion that the Bible actually "speaks." The biblical text does nothing as it lies closed upon a table; it has no voice until it is embodied in the voice of a reader/interpreter. The Bible does not speak; people *using* the Bible speak.

His next chapter critiques proponents of the traditional historical-critical method who attempt to pass off their own biased readings as simply "what the Bible clearly says." If the Bible "clearly" or unequivocally conveys its meaning, then how is it that we need interpreters in the first place? Furthermore, how is it that two equally faithful, equally intelligent, equally disciplined historical-critical exegetes using the same interpretive tool kit can and often do arrive at diametrically opposed interpretations?

Readers and Reading Communities?

Stanley Fish, the literary critic who became famous for his work *Is There a Text in This Class? The Authority of Interpretive Communities* (1980), taught us to regard seriously the role of interpretive communities in deriving or creating meaning from texts. The reading process is a complex, rich, multifaceted event that occurs between at least the text and its readers, a conversation (or struggle) that may produce multiple meanings from a given biblical text.

But some people worry that if meaning doesn't inhere concretely and absolutely in the text, then "it's all just relative" and the interpretive process devolves into nothing more than a "slippery slope" of people just making the Bible say whatever they want it to say. This may simply be a negative way to render my statement above about the "rich, multifaceted event." Perhaps better said, whether you identify more with statement one (multifaceted interpretation) or two (absolute interpretation) probably depends on whether you sympathize with a postmodernist approach (statement one) or a modernist one (statement two).

You, the Reader(s)

The people who *wrote* the Bible were socially located in a particular time and place, with certain views of the cosmos, of the nature of human beings, of gender, of politics, and so on. We do well to attend to this fact when interpreting the Bible.

People who *read* the Bible are socially located in a particular time and place, with certain views of the cosmos, of the nature of human beings, of gender, of politics, and so on. We do well to attend to this fact when interpreting the Bible.

Analogously, consider how the historical boundedness of authors and readers has impacted the interpretation of the American Constitution over the centuries. The Constitution was written by white, landed, male aristo-crats and (initially) was interpreted only by the same. Back in the day, a white male interpreted it to mean that slavery was fine and slaves were not equal. African Americans and women were excluded and had no access to rights or even full personhood. So if you were black or female, and worse, black *and* female, the Constitution may not have struck you as a great stride in human history. Shall we say that the Constitution was thoroughly bad and useless? No, but we must say it was, and continues to be, constrained by its time. As the guiding moral, legal, and political document of American society, it is always being discussed, debated, interpreted, and where necessary, amended due to new knowledge and advances in human thinking. As a result, African Americans and women eventually secured the right to vote and participate in the American political process; they have even gained the right to act as official interpreters of the document that once excluded them. We have des-ignated official interpreters of the Constitution even today because we know that it is a living document that must be engaged, tested, and challenged in an ongoing, critical fashion if we are to create a just society. Is this not also the case with our Scriptures?

I often invite my students to complete a hermeneutical self-inventory that helps them become at least partially aware of what they bring to the text as interpreters. It may be useful for you to think through these questions for yourself before proceeding.[9]

HERMENEUTICAL SELF-INVENTORY

1. *Church history*: How does my denominational history and tradition factor into my interpretation of the Bible, if at all?

2. *Authoritative criteria*: What are the norms or standards *beyond* the Bible that my tradition consults to determine how the Bible functions as the Word of God? Is it a person (John Calvin for Presbyterians, John Wesley for Meth-odists, Roger Williams and Anne Hutchison for American Baptists, the Pope for Catholics, Joseph Smith for Mormons, Martin Luther for Lutherans, etc.)? Is it a church body? A confession? A creed? A set of customs? A type of personal experience (dramatic conversion, speaking in tongues, snake han-dling)? A social commitment?

9. This inventory is based upon Norman Gottwald's chapter "Framing Biblical Interpreta-tion at New York Theological Seminary: A Student Self-Inventory on Biblical Hermeneutics," in *Reading from This Place*, vol. 1, *Social Location and Biblical Interpretation in the United States*, ed. Fernando F. Segovia and Mary Ann Tolbert (Minneapolis: Fortress, 1995), 251–61; the ques-tions are from 257–61.

3. *Default theology*: "What is my actual working theology regarding interpretation of the Bible? To what extent is this the same or different from the official position of my denomination or the 'average' viewpoint among my church associates? Is my working theology more or less the same as my formal theology, such as I might state in an application to a seminary or before a church body?"

4. *Ethnicity*: "How does my ethnic history, culture, and consciousness influence my interpretation of the Bible?"

5. *Gender*: "How does my gender history, culture, and consciousness influence my interpretation of the Bible?"

6. *Social class*: "How does my social-class history, culture, and consciousness influence my interpretation of the Bible? Since the dominant ideology in our society tends to deny that social classes exist among us, or to belittle the significance of class, it may take considerable effort on your part to identify your class location. For starters, you can ask about work experience, inherited wealth, income, education, types of reading, news sources consulted, social and career aspirations, and so on, and you can ask these questions about yourself, your parents, your grandparents, your associates, your neighborhood, your church."

7. *Education*: "How does my level and type of education influence my interpretation of the Bible? If I have had technical or professional training in non-religious fields, how does this impact my way of reading the Bible?"

8. *Community priorities*: "How do the values, welfare, and survival needs recognized or felt implicitly in my community/church influence my interpretation of the Bible?"

9. *Explicit political stance*: "How does my avowed political position influence my biblical interpretation? Politics is about as narrowly conceived in this country as is class. The term 'political position' in this question refers to more than political party affiliation or location on a left-right political spectrum. It also takes into account how much impact one feels from society and government on one's own life, and how much responsibility one takes for society and government, and in what concrete ways. Also involved is how one's immediate community/church is oriented toward sociopolitical awareness."

10. *Implicit political stance*: Even if I don't consider myself politically involved, "how does this 'nonpolitical' attitude and stance influence my biblical interpretation? What is the implicit political stance of my church and of other religious people with whom I associate?"

11. *Bible exposure*: "How does the mix of uses of the Bible to which I have been or am currently exposed influence my biblical interpretation? Such uses may include worship, preaching, church-school instruction, private study, Bible school training, ethical and theological resourcing, solitary or group devotions or spiritual exercises, and so on."

12. *Bible translations*: "How do the Bible translations and study Bibles I use influence my interpretation of the Bible? What translation(s) do I regularly or frequently use, and why? If I use a particular study Bible with explanatory essays and notes, what line of interpretation is expressed in it? Do I accept the study Bible interpretations without question or do I consult other sources of information to compare with them?"

13. *Resources*: "How do the published resources I regularly or sometimes consult influence my biblical interpretation? Among these resources may be one's private library, a church or seminary library, periodicals, church-school educational materials, sermon helps, and so on."

14. *Why preach? Why listen?* "How do my church and pastor (or myself as pastor) understand the role of the Bible in preaching as an aspect of the mission of the church, and how does that understanding influence my own pattern of biblical interpretation?"

15. *Attitude toward biblical scholarship*: "How does my attitude toward and use or nonuse of biblical scholarship influence my biblical interpretation? Am I inclined automatically to accept or to reject whatever a biblical scholar claims? Does the biblical scholarship I am familiar with increase or decrease my sense of competence and satisfaction with biblical study?"

16. *Family influence*: "What was the characteristic view of the Bible in my childhood home? Have I stayed in continuity with that view? Do I now see the Bible rather differently than my parents did (or do)? If there have been major changes in my view of the Bible, how did these come about? How do I feel about differences in biblical understanding within my current family setting?"

17. *Life crises*: "Have I experienced crises in my life in which the Bible was a resource or in which I came to a deeper or different understanding of the Bible than I had held before? If so, what has been the lasting effect of the crisis on my biblical interpretation?"

18. *Spirituality or divine guidance*: "What has been my experience of the role of the Bible in spiritual awareness or guidance from God? What biblical language and images play a part in my spiritual awareness and practice? How do I relate this 'spiritual' use of the Bible to other ways of reading and interpreting the Bible? Do these different approaches to the Bible combine comfortably for me or are they in tension or even open conflict?"

19. *Mixing and prioritizing these factors*: "Now that I have attended to each of these hermeneutical factors, is it possible to rank them in terms of the extent of their importance in my biblical interpretation? Do I recognize that some factors are 'foundational' or 'pivotal' for me? If that seems to be so, how are the less dominant factors related to and affected by the more dominant factors? Do I detect any factor at work in my biblical interpretation that is not

identified in the self-inventory? Does it surprise me to find that some factors are apparently more influential in my biblical interpretation than I had previously realized?"

20. *Next steps*: "What new awareness do I gain from this self-inventory as to how I actually interpret the Bible as the particular person I am? Do I want to learn more about the workings of some of these hermeneutical factors in the way I interpret? Now that I am getting more aware of how these factors interplay in my interpretation, is there anything I may want to consider changing in my attitude or practice so that I may become a more adequate and self-consistent biblical interpreter?"

A CANON WITHIN A CANON?

Most of us who care a lot about the Bible operate with some version of a "canon within the canon" that colors the way we view the rest of the Bible, not to mention our lives of piety more broadly. Many of us don't even know that we are doing this, privileging one or a cluster of texts over all others. Recently, Dr. Carolyn J. Sharp of Yale Divinity School asked her students to answer the following question:

> John R. Franke writes of Karl Barth, "Barth's work can be read as an attempt to see all things connected in Christ through an extended commentary on the biblical proclamation that 'in Christ God was reconciling the world to himself (2 Cor. 5:19)' (*Barth for Armchair Theologians*, 137). If you had to choose a single verse or phrase from the Hebrew Scriptures on which you would base your entire life's work as a minister or scholar (or activist or artist—whatever is true for you), what would that verse or phrase be and why?

Students shared their answers and they were written up on a whiteboard. It was a rich, even moving, experience for the gathered group as they were able, in her words, "to glimpse into the life narratives and deepest convictions of the students in the class." How would you answer my colleague's question yourself, dear reader? What if you did this exercise with those in your church?

We might argue that Martin Luther's canon within the canon was Galatians 2:16 (which is echoed in a number of verses in Romans): "Yet we know that a person is justified not by the works of the law but through faith in Jesus Christ." He read the Bible through the lens of justification by faith. Some traditions whose main focus is the salvation of individual sinners to gain entrance into heaven and avoid eternal hell appeal to a group of seven verses known as the "Roman Road."[10] Practitioners of snake-handling liturgies rely upon Mark 16:17–20:

> And these signs will accompany those who believe: by using my name they will cast out demons; they will speak in new tongues; they will pick up snakes in their hands, and if they drink any deadly thing, it will not hurt them; they will lay their hands on the sick, and they will recover." So then the Lord Jesus, after he had spoken to them, was taken up into heaven and sat down at the right hand of God. And they went out and proclaimed the good news everywhere, while the Lord worked with them and confirmed the message by the signs that accompanied it.

Interpreters who intuit their life's work to be liberation of the oppressed may be strongly guided by verses such as these:

> When he [Jesus] came to Nazareth, where he had been brought up, he went to the synagogue on the sabbath day, as was his custom. He stood up to read, and the scroll of the prophet Isaiah was given to him. He unrolled the scroll and found the place where it was written:
>
> "The Spirit of the Lord is upon me,
>   because he has anointed me to bring good news to the poor.
> He has sent me to proclaim release to the captives
>   and recovery of sight to the blind,
>   to let the oppressed go free,
> to proclaim the year of the Lord's favor."
>
> (Luke 4:16–19)
>
> But let justice roll down like waters,
>   and righteousness like an ever-flowing stream.
> (Amos 5:24–25)
>
> He has told you, O mortal, what is good;
>   and what does the LORD require of you
> but to do justice, and to love kindness,
>   and to walk humbly with your God?"
> (Mic. 6:8–9)

What passages are meaningful to you?

SAMPLE EXERCISE: MATTHEW 15:21–28

What would it look like if we applied our conversation from this chapter to a brainstorming session on Matthew 15:21–28?

10. See http://contenderministries.org/romanroad.php.

> Jesus left that place and went away to the district of Tyre and Sidon. Just then a Canaanite woman from that region came out and started shouting, "Have mercy on me, Lord, Son of David; my daughter is tormented by a demon." But he did not answer her at all. And his disciples came and urged him, saying, "Send her away, for she keeps shouting after us." He answered, "I was sent only to the lost sheep of the house of Israel." But she came and knelt before him, saying, "Lord, help me." He answered, "It is not fair to take the children's food and throw it to the dogs." She said, "Yes, Lord, yet even the dogs eat the crumbs that fall from their masters' table." Then Jesus answered her, "Woman, great is your faith! Let it be done for you as you wish." And her daughter was healed instantly.

Traditional interpretation might emphasize either Jesus' power to heal people, or the importance of faith in being healed, his "testing" of the woman's faith, or the way that Jesus the Jew, going against the natural grain of his religion, widens the circle a bit to include Gentiles. But could this story be read differently?

The narrative first notes that Jesus went to the region of Tyre and Sidon, which indeed is Gentile territory, outside the land of Israel. The passage is rich with potential for postcolonial analysis as it is rife with political, economic, racial, and ethnic boundary issues. Clearly Israel is privileged in this story, and the unnamed woman is painted as the "undeserving other," a foreigner (even though Jesus is outside of his own country), someone who is "lesser than." She brings nothing to the table; Jesus deigns to provide a handout from his abundance. It's not enough, apparently, for Matthew to call her a Gentile; rather, he designates her a "Canaanite." This is, of course, a historical anachronism since the Canaanites lived many centuries ago and were driven out (killed, assimilated) by the imperializing conquerors, in this case the Israelites. Hence, to call the woman a Canaanite is to further degrade and marginalize her. Furthermore, Jesus tells her flat out that his power and product is to be used to benefit *only* those of his own nation. This should not surprise the reader since he has already told the disciples in the Missionary Discourse of chapter 10 to "Go nowhere among the Gentiles, and enter no town of the Samaritans, but go rather to the lost sheep of the house of Israel" (10:6).

Not only is this woman not a member of the "house of Israel," she also is male-less, which in her culture (and perhaps in most cultures today) leaves her exceedingly vulnerable. Without a male, there's no money; without money, there's little access to health care. Without a male of her own, a woman is often left no choice but to get on her knees and throw herself upon the mercy of another male. How terrifying, then, when Jesus, the foreign male she is desperately and shamefully begging from (and not even for her own sake but for the sake of one even more vulnerable than she, a female child), first rebuffs her with silence. What does his silence mean? Will he harm her, kick her as she's down in the dirt debasing herself, groveling, making herself as small as possible so that he is bigger and taller and can look down upon her as she piles up honorific titles fit for an emperor or a king (note the reference to David)? Will he simply ignore her and thereby destroy her last hope?

As if that weren't threatening enough, now a whole pack of males (Jesus' disciples) turn against her, and Jesus makes the comment about his patriotism to Israel. Still, she presses on, having nothing left to lose. Jesus then makes another racial slur that literally dehumanizes her. Israelites are children; her kind are mere curs. Sometimes interpreters try to soften Jesus' words by noting that that the diminutive form of the word dog is used here. But as one scholar said, there's not a lot of difference between "bitch" and "little bitch."[11] The context in which Jesus makes the comment is polemical, not warm and cuddly. For the sake of her daughter, she absorbs the slur and even adopts it so as to protect herself and her daughter. She has no power and is in an extremely compromising situation—now is not the time to fight back.

But as a matter of fact, she is fighting back by "using the master's tools to dismantle his house." Hers is a subversive approach, and women worldwide as well as groups like African Americans who were enslaved in America have been relying on such techniques for centuries. And sometimes it works. By the end of this story, the woman has taught Jesus a lesson about his own identity and mission that even he himself didn't know (let alone his ill-mannered disciples)—that his mission was broader than he had realized. Jesus, it turns out, is not a flat literary character; he develops, with her help. Her grit and wit literally saved her and her daughter. She is the only hero in the story. You might say she is a protofeminist.

Women and children have always been disproportionately represented among the poor. Women still do the majority of the world's labor and own hardly any of the world's goods. In this story, gender, race, ethnicity, culture, politics, and disability intertwine. The woman has a sick child and seems to have no one to rely on. Women tend to be assigned the care of those who are sick, thus further inhibiting their ability to sustain a profitable job that could lead to independence and agency. In this story, the daughter is said to be "tormented by a demon." Disability theorists would have us unpack this. What did it mean in its own context? Certainly ancient medical models have little in common with current ones. Does she have a sickness, an illness, a disease (these are not synonyms)? Is this a physical ailment? A mental illness? Is it a short-term or chronic condition? Does it incapacitate the daughter

11. Amy-Jill Levine, "Matthew's Advice to a Divided Readership," in *The Gospel of Matthew in Current Study*, ed. David E. Aune (Grand Rapids: Wm. B. Eerdmans Pub. Co., 2001), 32.

such that she cannot easily be integrated into society, be a "productive" citizen, hold a job, have a family? How old is this daughter? Can she worship with her community, or must she remain sequestered according to her society's mores?

Just as the language of illness is debated, so is the language of health. What does it mean to be healed or cured? How is that different from being saved, if at all? When the woman with the issue of blood was made well in Matthew 9:22, Matthew uses the Greek word *sōzō*, typically translated as "save." Indeed, Jesus was to be named "Jesus" because he was to "save [*sōzō*] his people from their sins" (Matt. 1:21). Why, then, do we hear in 15:28 that the woman's daughter was "cured" (Greek: *iaomai*)? Was there something different about the result of the miracle in chapter 9 versus chapter 15? Furthermore, can one be saved without being cured? Can one be both "whole" and disabled? Is the language literal, metaphorical, both? How did her being healed affect her life on the ground—her relationships with friends, enemies, family; her sense of self; her identity; her relationship with God; her place in her religious community; her place in her society and its economy? One crucial question: what does her story teach us to ask about our own context with respect to persons with disabilities?

POWER AND ACCOUNTABILITY IN
BIBLICAL INTERPRETATION

Any conversation about the politics of biblical interpretation has to ask about power and accountability. We have wondered together about where the power of interpretive "meaning" lies—with the author, the text, the readers and reading communities, or somewhere in the interaction of all of these agents? There is also the question of the power of the interpreter to persuade others who regard the texts as sacred. Who gets to speak on behalf of the Bible? Whose voice matters most and on what basis? This is a crucial question for me as a heavily credentialed interpreter. I am credentialed both by the American Baptist Churches USA as well as by the academy through my earning a PhD from Yale. I preach from pulpits and teach Bible studies in churches. I am a seminary professor who lectures to students, chooses what they must read, and evaluates their interpretive work. Dr. Robert Foster recently engaged a number of seminary professors in deliberation over our role as professors and how we wield our power in the process of teaching the Bible. He labeled the discussion "Is There a Professor in This Class?"—an obvious reference to the Fish book alluded to earlier. One of the discussants broadened the conversation and titled her thread "And Are There Students in

This Class?" Structures of power have always mattered for the ways the Bible gets interpreted and proclaimed.

It is exceedingly important, then, to consider how (or if) interpreters are ethically accountable for the effects of the interpretations that they espouse. By what standards should any given interpretation be judged? If your pastor interprets the Bible in a sermon in a way that leads her or him to tell your congregation tomorrow to go and destroy a local mosque or murder a doctor who performs abortions, how would your church respond? If it sought to contradict the pastor's interpretation, upon what basis would it do so? Would it adduce other, different Scriptures, or appeal to other epistemological or ethical principles of "truth," or all of the above?

The *politics* of biblical interpretation is necessarily bound to the *ethics* of biblical interpretation. "By acknowledging the pervasiveness and unavoidability of ideologies, good and bad, biblical interpreters in our rhetorical contexts can choose simply to 'play' with texts and market entertaining readings that 'sell,' or we can assume responsibility to persuade one another and our communities and nations about matters vital to us all through interpretations of biblical texts that have transformed us."[12] I hope that the book you are holding in your hand invites you into deep, transformative play with our biblical texts. Here's my closing bumper-sticker thought: INTERPRET RESPONSIBLY.

---

12. Beverly Stratton, "Ideology," in *Handbook of Postmodern Biblical Interpretation*, ed. A. K. M. Adam (St. Louis: Chalice Press, 2000), 127.

Scripture Index

Subject Index